MORENO VALLEY
FEB 05 2002

D0478600

WOMEN
IN ANCIENT
EGYPT

WOMEN
IN ANCIENT
EGYPT

Barbara
Watterson

A Sutton Publishing Book

This edition published in 1998 by Wrens Park Publishing, an imprint of
W.J. Williams & Son Ltd

This book was designed and produced by
Alan Sutton Publishing Limited, an imprint of Sutton Publishing Limited
Phoenix Mill · Thrupp · Stroud · Gloucestershire GL5 2BU

Copyright © Barbara Watterson, 1991

All rights reserved. No part of this publication may be reproduced, stored in a
retrieval system, or transmitted, in any form or by any means, electronic,
mechanical, photocopying, recording or otherwise, without the prior
permission of the publishers and copyright holder.

A catalogue record for this book is available from the British Library

ISBN 0 905 778 235

Typeset in 11/14 Baskerville.
Typesetting and origination by
Sutton Publishing Limited.
Printed in Great Britain by
WBC Limited, Bridgend, Mid-Glamorgan

CONTENTS

List of Illustrations   vii

Introduction   ix

Chapter One   **Ancient Egyptian Attitudes Towards Women**   1

Chapter Two   **Women in Society: I**   23
Social and Legal Position

Chapter Three   **Women in Society: II**   35
Female Occupations and Professions

Chapter Four   **Love and Marriage**   54

Chapter Five   **Health and Childbirth**   73

Chapter Six   **Dress and Adornment**   94

Chapter Seven   **Domestic Life**   120

Chapter Eight   **Women of Power**   137

References   173

Index of Ancient Egyptian Words and Phrases   194

General Index   195

In memory of my father

LIST OF ILLUSTRATIONS

COLOUR PLATES
(*between pages 78 and 79*)

1   Cosmetic vase
2   Ramesses III and daughters
3   Statue of Hatshepsut
4   Hunting in marshes
5   Spinning and weaving
6   Servant statue
7   Guests at feast
8   Musicians and dancers
9   Dresses
10 Bread-maker servant statue
11 Necklace
12 Hair pin
13 Elysian fields

BLACK AND WHITE ILLUSTRATIONS

1   Cutting wheat today, Qurna, Luxor   xii
2   Ploughing relief   xiii
3   Cutting wheat   xiv
4   Seneb statue   3
5   Ankhnesmeryre and Pepi II statue   6
6   Ramesses II and daughter   7
7   Female sculpture   9
8   Isis and Horus statue   20
9   Servants' relief   36
10 *Sistrum*   41
11 *Menit*-necklace   42

12	Widow casting dust on head	45
13	Mourners	46
14	Acrobatic dancers	48
15	Acrobatic dancer	48
16	Lute player	51
17	Musicians	52
18	Bes statue	93
19	Old Kingdom style of dress and wig	98
20	New Kingdom style of dress	100
21	Paddle doll, wood and beads	101
22	New Kingdom style of wig	103
23	Queen Kawit	114
24	Neferu and servant hairdressing	114
25	Unguent spoon	118
26	Mother and baby	123
27	Beer-making servant statue	131
28	Drawing of Cleopatra	142
29	Relief of Cleopatra	144
30	Cleopatra, contemporary head	146
31	Cleopatra, coin	147
32	Queen Tiy	150
33	Nefertiti	152
34	Amarna princess	153
35	Nefertiri	155
36	Nefertiri and Isis	156
37	Temple of Divine Votaresses	161
38	Ramesses III	162
39	Shepenwepet I	163
40	Amenirdis I	164

INTRODUCTION

History has traditionally been concerned primarily with the affairs and deeds of kings and rulers and only in recent years have scholars begun to study and write about 'ordinary' people to any great extent. The role of women, who can be said to be 'the other half of history', has often been overlooked. In this book an attempt has been made to redress the balance for the women who lived in Egypt during the pharaonic period, that is, the period from *c*. 3100 BC to 30 BC, using written, monumental and artistic sources, including, when appropriate, those from the Graeco-Roman era post 30 BC and from modern times.

Although the civilization that flourished on the banks of the Nile for some 3,000 years before Christ has left behind more visible and tangible remains than any other, evidence for any aspect of life as lived in ancient Egypt tends, nevertheless, to be fragmentary. Such evidence as there is comes from three principal sources: monuments; papyri and ostraca; and the accounts given by contemporary Greek and Roman travellers.

Inscriptions, reliefs and sculptures in temples are almost wholly of a religious nature, concerned with the worship of the gods, and occasionally recording the exploits of kings. They are, therefore, of limited value in reconstructing aspects of Egyptian society that are of a secular nature. Tombs on the other hand are an altogether better source. It is true that the theme of many of the reliefs carved or painted on their walls is religious, but in tombs from every period of ancient Egyptian history, scenes from the home life of the deceased are depicted. Statues are found in tombs and they, at the very least, give an indication of the styles of dress, hair and adornment worn by the ancient Egyptians. In addition, numerous objects of everyday life, either actual examples or models, were buried in the tomb. The poorer classes could not afford tombs but were instead buried in graves dug in the desert sand. Even these, however, contain grave goods in the form of knives, pots and jewellery.

The bodies of the dead, whether buried in tombs or graves, yield an invaluable amount of information. Mummification, that is, the preservation of the dead body by artificial means, was practised in Egypt from about 2600 BC to the fourth century AD. Generally speaking, only those who could afford tombs were mummified; but the dry Egyptian climate has desiccated the bodies of the poorer classes who were interred in simple graves, turning them into natural mummies. In recent years, the examination of mummies has become a multi-disciplinary activity; some of them have even been used for molecular cloning of their DNA. Studies such as that undertaken by the Manchester Mummy Research Team have disclosed, among other things, much valuable information about disease and living conditions in all classes of ancient Egyptian society.

The amount of contemporary written evidence on papyri and ostraca (pieces of broken pot or flakes of limestone inscribed with written messages) varies according to period. As might be expected, what remains from the earlier periods of ancient Egyptian history is not as extensive as that which survives from the Graeco-Roman period; but tens of thousands of papyri, unfortunately not all of them complete, and thousands of ostraca, have been preserved, thanks to Egypt's hot, dry climate or through being buried in sand. The earliest written examples of papyrus are probably the fragments of temple account books from Abusir, now in the British Museum. There is a sizeable body of literature recorded on papyri, and an even larger number of business, legal and administrative documents, and wills. Ostraca, available in plenty at no cost, were used for scribblings and ephemera such as lists, school exercises and receipts.

Some of the most informative documents are written in demotic, 'the popular language' spoken in the Delta, which developed, towards the end of the seventh century BC, a distinct grammar and vocabulary of its own. It was written in a cursive script, also called demotic, and was used largely by lawyers and officials, who employed it in the writing of contracts, legal and administrative documents. The British Museum alone houses hundreds of demotic documents covering a period of some thousand years, from 643 BC to the middle of the fifth century AD.

The Egyptians began to use demotic in the reign of Psamme-tichus I, the first Egyptian king to invite Greek mercenaries to fight in his army. Greek traders soon followed their fellow Greeks to Egypt, and Greek settlements grew up there. A hundred years after the introduction of demotic, Egypt was invaded by the Persians (525 BC). Native kings regained control in 404; but in 343, the Persians were back again until driven out by Alexander the Great in 332. Alexander was eventually succeeded by the Ptolemaic dynasty of Macedonian Greek rulers who reigned in Egypt until, in 30 BC, Egypt became part of the Roman Empire. Thus, much of the information in demotic documents was written at a time when Egypt was under foreign domination. Although it is only to be expected that a good number of the documents should be con-cerned with the affairs of the ruling classes, who were largely Greek and Roman, such documents can nevertheless throw light upon conditions in pharaonic Egypt. As the great Egyptologist, Flinders Petrie (1821–1908), observed:

> There is such a close similarity between the Egyptians of those times (Greek and Roman) and the present – in spite of Christianity and Islam – that for the earlier ages of more uniform conditions we may well trust the late accounts of the classics.[1]

The three principal sources of evidence from contemporary Greek and Roman travellers in Egypt are the accounts given by Herodotus of Halicarnassus, Diodorus Siculus and Strabo. Hero-dotus, the 'Father of History', visited Egypt in about 450 BC, between August and November. He spoke no Egyptian and had to rely on local interpreters of doubtful competence and on fellow Greeks – merchants and mercenaries settled in Egypt – for much of his information; he was never in touch with higher circles of the administration and was totally unaware, for instance, that Aramaic was the administrative language of the country. He seems to have taken no notes on the spot, and Diodorus refers to 'all the casual inventions of Herodotus' (I,69). Nevertheless he was an inquisitive and diligent enquirer, and there is no reason to doubt that he recorded what he heard and saw faithfully. Strabo was in Egypt in 24 BC visiting his friend, the Roman Prefect, Aelius Gallus. Of the seventeen books of his great work on Geography one deals with Egypt. Diodorus Siculus, a celebrated Greek historian in the time of Julius Caesar and Augustus, travelled widely in Europe and Asia in the interests of making his History as complete and exact as possible: the section on Egypt contains not only an historical record but also information on art, medicine, language, literature and mummification.

It is a truism to say that the character of the inhabitants of a land is influenced by the nature of the land. Egypt has a total area of about 400,000 square miles, excluding the western oases and Sinai, of which less than 12,000 square miles was cultivable in pharaonic times – it is not much more than this today. In pharaonic times the cultivable land was in the Nile Valley and was provided by the

Cutting wheat today, Qurna, Luxor

actions of the Nile, which inundated its banks every year, thus irrigating the land with its water and fertilizing it with the silt that was left behind when the inundation abated, inspiring Herodotus's most famous observation, 'Egypt is the gift of the river'. The regularity of the inundation, the predictability of the climate and

> the more or less geographical isolation of this narrow, fertile Nile valley, has produced a conservative people who, in spite of conquering invaders in the past, have retained to a remarkable extent very many of their ancient customs, beliefs and industries, adapting the older beliefs and rites to the Christian and Islamic faiths, and preserving many of their social customs practically unchanged from ancient times.[2]

Winifred Blackman made the foregoing observation in the 1920s, and anyone travelling around Egypt today, observing the life led by the *fellahin*, the agricultural workers who make up over 50 per cent of the population, would be forced to the same conclusions. For more than a decade Egyptian farmers have increasingly made use of modern technology, working their land using tractors, threshing machines and fertilizers; but the use of modern machinery and methods is far outweighed by the continuing use of the traditional ways of ploughing with wooden ploughs drawn by

Ploughing relief from *mastaba*-tomb of Nefer, Sakkara, Old Kingdom

Cutting wheat, from the tomb of Menna, Thebes, Eighteenth
Dynasty

animals, cutting wheat with hand scythes, and winnowing by
tossing up the wheat into the air for the wind to blow away the
chaff. The difference between Egypt and other countries is that
these and other activities practised in Egypt today can be seen
depicted on the walls of tombs from pharaonic Egypt (Pl. 13). There
have been a few changes. Tomb-paintings depict wheat being
threshed by animals driven over a threshing-floor; today a device
called a *nurag*, which is a sort of wooden chair set on runners, is
used. But there are more similarities than changes. And the beliefs
and customs that survived from pharaonic Egypt, especially as far
as the women of rural Egypt were concerned, to the Egypt Winifred
Blackman recorded, can still be found in rural Egypt today. The
history of the past can teach us about our present; in Egypt the
present can often teach us about the past.

CHAPTER ONE

ANCIENT EGYPTIAN ATTITUDES TOWARDS WOMEN

In modern Western society it is comparatively recent that long-held prejudices and assumptions about women have been questioned and challenged. At school little girls have traditionally been expected to play with dolls and model kitchens – girls' toys – while boys play with soldiers. Boys have been expected to study woodwork, girls needlework; boys to specialize in science, girls in arts subjects. Nursing, teaching and secretarial work have been deemed suitable careers for women while men become doctors, pilots, captains of industry. Changing attitudes towards women and raising their expectations is a long, difficult and continuing process. Women today have gone beyond the confines of *Kinder, Küche and Kirche* but many male attitudes towards them are deeply ingrained, and even subconscious. It is surely not unreasonable to suppose that attitudes towards women in ancient Egypt were based on what was deemed to be their role in society and on how the female sex was perceived by men.

In ancient Egyptian society a woman was accorded legal rights equal to those of a man from the same social class and had the same expectation of a life after death. Such consideration towards women was rare in other ancient societies. Pharaonic Egypt was not an exclusively male-dominated society in which women were regarded by men merely as breeding machines or beasts of burden. Instead it was one in which they were allowed to exert a degree of freedom and, in some cases, influence, beyond the confines of the home, as we shall see in the following chapter. Nevertheless, an Egyptian woman's main occupations were marriage, running a household and bearing children, and inevitably the occupations of the majority

of women affected the status that men accorded them and con-
sequently affected male attitudes towards them. Throughout history men have been engaged in occupations outside the domestic
sphere and have played a part in public affairs. They have placed a
high value on their own activities and have been in a position to
persuade society that they deserve a higher status than women.
There is no reason to doubt that ancient Egyptian men viewed
themselves in this light.

It seems clear that many ancient Egyptian men indulged in
generalizations about the supposed characteristics of the female: a
wise remark was defined by a certain chief minister to the king as
one that 'could be understood even by women bending over the
grindstone'. Sinuhe, the hero of a famous story, described the
excitement as he was about to fight – 'Women, and even men,
jabbered!'; and among the graffiti on a temple wall is inscribed one
gem – 'As foolish as a woman's words'. However, assessing the
attitudes towards women held by ancient Egyptian society is
difficult. We are, of course, in no position at all to judge subconscious attitudes, and are forced largely to rely on evidence and
impressions gleaned from literary and artistic sources.

A great many visual representations of women survive from
ancient Egypt in the form of statues, reliefs and wall-paintings.
However, the Egyptian artist very rarely indulged in 'art for art's
sake', and almost every work produced was either for domestic use
as, for example, decorated pieces of furniture or jewellery; or for use
in a religious or funerary context. Statues were placed in tombs to
take the place of the dead body should it be damaged or destroyed,
as the preservation of the body was deemed necessary for a
continued existence in the Afterlife. Reliefs and paintings on the
walls of tombs were to enable the owner of the tomb to carry out the
activities they depicted in the Afterlife and once the correct magic
ritual had been carried out, statues and reliefs were believed to be
forever imbued with life. This magic ritual was known as the
'Opening of the Mouth' and during it a priest touched various parts
of the statue or relief with a ritual implement (an adze) reciting 'I
perform the Opening of the Mouth upon this your nose so that you
may breathe in the Afterlife. I perform the Opening of the Mouth

upon these your eyes so that you may see in the Afterlife', and so on.

Given the purposes of Egyptian art, the way in which women were depicted was not haphazard or, normally, left to the artist's discretion or inspiration. The owners of private tombs were usually men – women generally being buried with their nearest male relative. He was usually depicted as an athletic man, a perfect specimen in the prime of life, although in actuality he may have been quite the opposite. There were exceptions: for example, the statue of the famous dwarf, Seneb (*c.* 2530 BC), found in his tomb at Giza (and now in Cairo Museum), shows him as a dwarf although presumably he could have ordered the sculptor to present him as a

Seneb with his wife and children

normally-sized man. Like her husband, the wife of a tomb-owner was portrayed in an idealized fashion. In her case, however, she seems to be idealized not only by the conventions of Egyptian art but also by men's perceptions of women.

One convention was that in painted reliefs and statues a woman's flesh should be a creamy yellow, whereas for men it should be a reddish-brown. The creamy colour of women's flesh is probably to be taken as an indication that women had less exposure to the sun since they would have spent more time indoors or under shade engaged in 'women's activities', rather than as an indication of men's preference. Even so, the element of preference for a soft skin rather than one roughened by exposure to the elements is not to be dismissed.

According to another artistic convention the figure of the most important person in a relief should be the largest in it, and in many reliefs wives are depicted very much smaller in scale than their husbands: the husband, after all, was usually the tomb-owner. There are exceptions to this convention, especially among royal ladies who, presumably because of their royal status, achieved equal representation with their husbands. In many statue groups a man is represented with his wife, or with his wife and their children, or sometimes with his mother. Although the larger build of the man presumably reflected a real physical difference between the sexes, in some groups, particularly of the Old Kingdom, the distinction is very marked. The wife is depicted as literally 'the little woman', kneeling at her husband's feet and also sculpted on a much smaller scale than he. A less obvious way of indicating a wife's lower status is that in statue groups she is generally depicted sitting at her husband's left side, thought to be inferior to the right.

Individual statues of women are relatively rare, especially at the beginning of Egyptian history. One very fine example is the black granite life-sized statue of the Lady Sennuwy, dated to about 1950 BC, which was found in her tomb at Kerma in the Sudan (now in the Museum of Fine Arts, Boston). She sits on a stone block with her hands on her knees, with a confident and serene expression on her face. As this type of pose was normally reserved for men, one must suppose that Sennuwy was an unusually privileged lady.

Age, with its supposed accumulation of wisdom, was seen as a desirable quality in a man but not in a woman. Hence statues of men show them with rolls of fat around their midriffs, earned over many years of good living. Women on the other hand are represented as slim and youthful; and even the mother of a man, when she appears in tomb depictions with his wife, appears to be the same age as what, in most cases, must have been the younger woman.

In tomb reliefs the wife, or sometimes the mother, of the deceased is always depicted in a formal manner, usually seated at his side. She is never represented in an undignified manner; but then, of course, neither is he. Only servants, workmen and foreigners are represented informally, the servants and workmen going about their everyday work. Thus servant women are depicted spinning, weaving, making bread and beer and performing menial tasks: the lady of the house sits at leisure in her elegant dress on a chair or a stool. Occasionally she is depicted accompanying her husband as he observes his men at work – standing a few steps behind him. Whenever a woman is shown alongside her husband, whether in statue or relief, she generally has her arm around his waist or over his shoulder: an indication that her role was to be one of encouragement and support.

Statues and reliefs depicting women were sometimes placed in temples. Ancient Egyptian temples were of two types: those concerned with the mortuary cult of the dead monarch (usually a king, but see Chapter Eight), and those dedicated to the worship of one or more gods – cult temples. In both types, reliefs depicting the king making offerings to the gods were sculpted on the walls, and statues of kings were erected, those in cult temples especially put there in order to associate the king more closely with the god. Sometimes the queen is shown in the reliefs playing a secondary role in the making of offerings: it is very seldom that she takes the leading role (but see Nefertiti, page 154). In some temples, statues of queens were erected but these always show them in a secondary role. One of the earliest (*c.* 2260 BC) is that of Ankhnesmeryre, the mother of Pepi II. This alabaster statue, which is now in the Brooklyn Museum, probably came from Pepi's mortuary temple at Sakkara. It shows Ankhnesmeryre, in large scale, as a mother, with

Ankhnesmeryre and Pepi II statue

the boy king, in realistic small scale, on her lap. Later on statues of
other queens were erected in cult temples, placed there by their
husbands as a mark of favour: at Luxor, for example, the queens
and daughters of Ramesses II (1304–1238 BC) are depicted in some
statue groups, sculpted in small scale against the leg of the king; at
Medinet Habu the wives and daughters of Ramesses III (1198–1166
BC) are treated in the same way (Pl. 2). There are examples of
private persons dedicating statues of themselves to cult temples;
occasionally, women figure in this category. The black granite bust
of an unknown early Twelfth Dynasty lady (about 1991–1962 BC),
now in the Brooklyn Museum, is one such.

Ramesses II and daughter, Luxor temple

Artistic evidence that women were viewed as sexual objects is not overt: the Egyptians were in any case discreet in their artistic representations of contact with the opposite sex and there are very few depictions of a couple embracing let alone indulging in copulation. There is only one obscene document known so far. This is a papyrus,[1] dating to about 1150 BC, on which is a set of cartoons, with captions, depicting fat, bald, priapic men in a succession of sexual encounters with one or more women. Similar encounters are the subjects of many ostraca found at the workmen's village at Deir el-Medina (see page 191); and presumably there must have been others elsewhere which have not survived.

In many reliefs women are shown with their husbands in seemingly innocuous situations – sitting listening to the playing of musical instruments, perhaps with a pet monkey or a goose under the chair, the woman holding a lotus flower and wearing a heavy wig; or out hunting in the marshes (Pl. 4) with a duck perched on the front of the skiff. These reliefs, however, contain coded erotic references. The wig had erotic associations; so did the monkey, the duck and the goose, which some think were related to female sexuality. The lotus meant to the Egyptians what a red rose means to us. Even the musical instruments could have erotic significance. The use of erotic motifs became common only in the New Kingdom, and one famous Eighteenth Dynasty relief, now in the British Museum, illustrates the genre well. The relief comes from the tomb of a Theban nobleman named Nebamun, who lived around 1412–1402 BC. In it he is depicted out hunting in the marshes with his wife and daughter. His wife, smaller than her husband, stands behind him wearing a diaphanous, elaborately pleated dress and a long, heavy wig – not at all the sort of costume for a day's fowling. In her hands she grasps a *sistrum* (see page 40) and necklace, both associated with Hathor, the goddess of love. On the front of the skiff a duck is perched – perhaps to be interpreted as simply a refugee from the hunting, but perhaps a symbol of her sexuality.

Such scenes were designed to provide an erotic ambience for the male tomb-owner. However the depiction of women as sex objects was not simply for a man's pleasure: sexuality was deemed important because of its association with birth and fertility. In tombs it took on a religious aspect because of its extended association with creation and rebirth in the Afterlife. It is interesting to note that it is the woman who is expected to make herself attractive to the man, and not the other way round – a reflection perhaps of the fact that, as in most societies, men considered that women were for their delectation and that sexuality in women was only permissible when it was at the service of men.

Egyptian literature, of which a considerable body survives, can help fill out the picture of male perceptions of women. Love poetry complements the evidence of the artistic representations: extolling the physical attributes of a woman was as much a favourite theme of ancient Egyptian poetry as it has always been of the poetry of other times and places. The following extract taken from a love poem illustrates what was, for most Egyptian men, the ideal of feminine beauty. It is the same ideal that is portrayed in sculpture and painting: a woman should be graceful and slim, with a small waist and small, firm breasts, a long neck, a pale skin and blue-black hair.

> Of surpassing radiance and luminous skin,
> With lovely, clear-gazing eyes,
> Her lips speak sweetly
> With not a word too much.

Bust of woman, Twelfth Dynasty

> Her neck is long, her breast is white,
> Her hair is true lapis lazuli.
> Her arm surpasses gold
> And her fingers are like lotus buds.
> With rounded thighs and trim waist,
> Her legs display her beauty when,
> With graceful gait, she treads the earth.[2]

Most ancient Egyptians were illiterate, so that even the love poetry, which seems to be so personal, was actually the work of official scribes and as such was recognized as a formal part of ancient Egyptian literature. The basic love poem takes the form of an address to the heart or to the loved one made in the first person; and the lovers in the poems address each other as 'brother' or 'sister', the conventional ancient Egyptian terms of endearment, not to be taken literally. The following poem illustrates the point perfectly:

> My god, my husband, I come to you.
> It is pleasant to go into the pool and
> I rejoice that you wish me
> To plunge in and bathe before you.
> I let you see my beauty
> In a tunic of fine royal linen
> When it is wet.
> I go into the water with you
> And emerge with a red fish for you
> Pulsating in my hands.
> I lay it on my breast.
> O my man, my brother,
> Come and see me!

At first glance the above poem seems to indicate that the status of ancient Egyptian women was such that the speaker in a poem could be female; that it was just as acceptable for her to use erotic imagery in the expression of her feelings as it was for a man. On the other hand it is feasible that it was only male fantasy to suppose that women would express themselves in the phrases used in the poem. Since women did not actually write the poems it is tantalizing to conjecture what their feelings would really have been and how they would have expressed them.

Some poems reflect the state to which men suppose women can be reduced by the loved one, the mere sight of whom can distract a woman. As the following poem illustrates, when a woman sees her lover she forgets even what men are pleased to imagine is her most important preoccupation, dressing her hair:

> My mind turned to my love for you
> When only half of my hair was plaited.
> I came running to find you
> And forgot about doing my hair.
> But if you will release me,
> I will finish dressing my hair
> And be ready in a minute!

A constant theme of ancient Egyptian love poems is the effect that love has on a woman. Love of a man is the source not only of a woman's happiness but also of her beauty:

> My heart is in accord with you.
> I do for you whatever it wishes
> When I am in your embrace.
> My desire for you is my eye-paint –
> Looking at you makes my eyes shine.
> I nestle close to you at seeing your love,
> O man who fills my heart.
> How pleasant is this time –
> May an hour last for eternity.
> Since I have been sleeping with you
> You have thrilled my heart.
> Whether I am sad or happy,
> Never leave me!

If love poetry presents women in a rosy, idealized light, then other forms of literature offer different stereotypes, many of which are far from flattering. Such views are often expressed in the *Wisdom Texts and Instructions*, a popular genre of ancient Egyptian literature, which can be an invaluable source of information on attitudes towards women. Some Egyptian men clearly took a somewhat cynical and jaundiced view of the opposite sex. One such was Ankhsheshonq,[3] a priest belonging to the temple of the sun god, Re, at Heliopolis, who is thought to have lived some time between 300 BC and 50 BC. In the advice that he gave to his son, Ankhsheshonq was scathing about the intellectual capabilities, morals and worth of women:

Let your wife see your wealth, but don't trust her with it.

Never send a mere woman on business for you – she will attend to her own first.

Never confide in your wife – what you say to her goes straight into the street.

Instructing a woman is like owning a sack of sand with a split in the side.

Don't glory in your wife's beauty – her heart is set on her lover.

What she does with her husband today she will do with another man tomorrow.

From the above it is clear that Ankhsheshonq considers women to be unfaithful, untrustworthy, incapable of learning or of keeping secrets.

Although some of Ankhsheshonq's sayings have a predictably familiar ring about them, and may be dismissed as what in modern parlance would be called 'male chauvinist pig remarks', it would be a mistake to take his less than flattering view of women as typical. In general women, or wives and mothers at least, were referred to in the more respectful terms such as those used by the sages Ptahhotep (see page 58) and Ani (see page 120). Ani's advice to a husband was:

Don't boss your wife in her own house when you know she is efficient. Don't keep saying to her 'Where is it? Bring it to me!' Especially when it is in the place where it ought to be!

A clear indication that Ani realized that men also have failings. Even Ankhsheshonq sometimes takes a less negative attitude:

A good woman of noble character [at least he admits that they exist] is food that comes in time of hunger.

Ankhsheshonq also admits that women have their uses:

The waste of a woman is not knowing [presumably in the Biblical sense] her.

A woman at night, praise by midday;

and, of course, he approves of mothers:

Open [your heart] to your mother – she is a woman of discretion.

May my mother be my hairdresser so as to do for me what is pleasant.

Many of the *Wisdom Texts and Instructions* give advice on how men should behave towards women. All seem to assume that there are three kinds of woman: the mother, the wife and the harlot. As we shall see in Chapter Seven, mothers are above reproach. Wives, on the other hand, fall into two categories: the good and faithful helpmeet, and the nagging gossip who is not only mercenary but also unfaithful. As for the harlot – a man finds it hard to ignore her but is advised to beware!

A set of maxims composed probably in the last century BC is contained in a demotic papyrus of the first century AD known as the Insinger Papyrus[4] (now in the Rijksmuseum, Leiden). Many of the maxims concern relations between the sexes:

Do not consort with a woman who consorts with your superior. If she is beautiful, keep away from her.

Some men dislike intercourse yet spend a fortune on women.

Even a wise man can be harmed by his love for a woman.

The fool who looks at a woman is like a fly on blood.

If a woman is beautiful you should show your superiority over her.

The work of Mut and Hathor is what acts among women. [Mut and Hathor were goddesses connected with love, the inference here being that women have no control over their emotions.]

The Insinger Papyrus merely confirms the impression given by the other *Wisdom Texts*: that the writers of these documents take a largely negative attitude towards women, viewing them as irrational, dangerous and needing to be dominated. It can only be hoped that the opinions of the writers of the *Texts* did not reflect male attitudes in general. Some small comfort may be derived from a final quotation from the Insinger Papyrus:

It is in women that both good and bad fortune are on earth.

Secular narratives throw further light on the stereotypes encountered in the *Wisdom* literature and elsewhere. In these tales it is men who are the heroes, the initiators of the action. Women play secondary roles, appearing for the most part as stubborn and unreasonable creatures, causing trouble through their vindictiveness or wicked behaviour. Numerous examples may be cited. The Westcar Papyrus,[5] for instance, dating to about 1674–1587 BC, relates the tale of how a bored King Sneferu decides to go for a boat trip in a craft rowed by twenty beautiful young women dressed only in nets. The king's pleasure is endangered by the stubborn behaviour of one of the oarswomen when she drops a prized turquoise pendant into the water. Unwilling to accept a replacement she brings the craft to a halt until the hero, Djadjaemankh, uses his magical powers to fold back the waters of the lake allowing the pendant to be retrieved. Another part of the same papyrus tells how a treacherous maidservant who betrays her mistress is, in punishment, carried off by a crocodile. This truly is a fate worse than death since her body would not have been available for proper burial and, thus, she would have been denied the benefit of an Afterlife. A similar fate befalls an adulterous wife in another of the Westcar tales.

Wicked, scheming or ambitious women appear in other stories and are the causes of the heroes' troubles. In the Story of the Two Brothers,[6] the temptress, who is not given a name, is the wife of the elder brother, Anubis – her character bears a marked resemblance to Potiphar's wife in the Biblical story of Joseph. In this tale, Anubis's wife conceives an illicit desire for her virtuous brother-in-law, Bata, whom she first tries to seduce and then, when he repulses her, falsely accuses of rape. Bata convinces his brother of his innocence, and Anubis kills his perfidious wife. The story continues, but Bata is destined to be unlucky with women. After many years of lonely exile, he is rewarded by the gods with a beautiful wife; but she is abducted by the king who makes her his Chief Favourite. A series of episodes follows in which the Chief Favourite betrays Bata, who is killed and returned to life several times, until finally he is reborn as the king's son. Bata inherits the throne and Anubis is made Crown Prince. At last the Chief Favourite is called to justice before the highest officials of the kingdom, who give their assent to whatever punishment Bata deems fit for her. The storyteller does not relate what the punishment is, but we can be sure it is not pleasant.

The hero of another story is also brought suffering by the machinations of a wicked woman, although in this case he is partly to blame for his predicament. He is Khamwese,[7] son of Ramesses II and High Priest of Ptah at Memphis. The story tells of how Khamwese, who was reputed to be a great magician, steals a magic book from the tomb of Neneferkaptah and his wife, despite the pleas of their spirits that the book should not be removed from the tomb. It is not long before Khamwese is brought to repent of his deeds by the actions of Tabubu, a beautiful woman whom he greatly desires. Tabubu promises herself to Khamwese but demands in return ever greater sacrifices from him, culminating in the murder of his children. Finally, just as he is about to bed

Tabubu, he wakes up and all is revealed as a horrible dream. Much chastened, Khamwese returns the book to the tomb. Although he has brought his troubles on himself by stealing from a tomb, it is perhaps instructive that the device by which Neneferkaptah brings Khamwese to heel is a beautiful but ruthless woman. One of the morals of this story is that even a wise man like Khamwese can fall prey to a beautiful woman's charms – a theme not unique to ancient Egyptian literature.

A rare example of a secular tale in which a woman takes a more active and positive role is that of the Doomed Prince.[8] In this story the prince hears that the King of Naharin has shut his daughter in a house with a window 70 cubits above the ground, and has promised her in marriage to whichever local prince is able to reach the window. The Doomed Prince, who gains the sympathy of the other contestants for the princess's hand by telling them, falsely but in true fairy-tale tradition, that he has left home on account of a wicked stepmother, succeeds in reaching the princess's window because this ancient Egyptian Rapunzel lets down her hair for him to use as a ladder. The Doomed Prince wins the love of the princess but the King of Naharin is reluctant to give his daughter to a man who is apparently a commoner; at this point, the princess makes a spirited intervention: 'If he is taken from me, I shall not eat, I shall not drink, I shall die at once!' and is forthwith given in marriage to the Doomed Prince. She proves to be of great help to her husband, watching over him to guard against the three Fates that she knows threaten him. One of the dangers – a snake – she dispatches personally by giving it wine and beer to drink and, when it rolls onto its back drunk, hacking it to pieces with an axe. The Doomed Prince's wife is an exceptional woman of action, a type rarely found in ancient Egyptian narrative tales.

If in secular tales women play only secondary roles – either as devoted mothers and faithful wives, or conversely as perfidious wives and wicked temptresses – in religious mythology these stereotyped images of women are somewhat less rigid. In certain respects, however, the roles played by Egyptian goddesses do correspond quite closely with the function of women in society. Women were wives and mothers, concerned with the well-being of their families; goddesses were consorts of gods and protectresses of mankind.

In ancient Egyptian religion there were a great many deities, both male and female. Every city, every town, originally every tribe in Egypt had its own gods and goddesses. In dynastic times kings and priests attempted to develop a unifying concept; hence every ruler promoted his own local god or personal deity to the position of state god, who was considered to be the primeval deity, ancestor of all the other gods. Their elevation to state god meant that these once merely local deities became universal gods with cult centres throughout Egypt. Thus, in the Old Kingdom (*c.* 2686–2181 BC) Re of Heliopolis was state god; in the New Kingdom (1551–1085 BC), and after, it was the turn of Amun of Thebes. Atum of Heliopolis, Ptah of Memphis and Horus of Edfu were also worshipped as universal deities. But Egypt never had a state goddess, although Isis and Hathor were universally worshipped. The great creator-gods were Atum, Ptah and Re; only one goddess, Neith, had her own creation legend. The great judges of the dead and gods of the Afterlife were Re, Anubis and Osiris; they had no female counter-parts. There were gods of war – Montu and Amun – but no goddesses, although several female deities, notably Sekhmet, Neith, Anat and Bastet, included warlike qualities in their natures.

In many cultures an Earth Mother plays a prominent role and is considered to be the most powerful of deities. In Egypt there was no earth goddess, only an earth god – Geb. There were, however, mother goddesses: the sky goddess, Nut, for example, or Amun's wife, Mut; above all, Osiris's wife, Isis. The chief deities concerned with fertility were male – Min, Osiris and Sobek being the most important. A lesser deity, Renenutet, was the only goddess to represent this concept. However, goddesses were the main repres-entatives of love and joy. There was no goddess – or god – of love, but several goddesses, notably Hathor and Bastet, included love among their aspects.

One of the most popular roles for a female deity was that of protectress. The cobra goddess, Edjo, was tutelary goddess of Lower Egypt; her Upper Egyptian counterpart was the vulture goddess Nekhbet. Isis, Nephthys, Neith and Serket had a funerary role, protecting the Canopic jars containing respectively the liver, lungs, stomach and intestines of the dead, or guarding the corners of shrines and sarcophagi. One or two goddesses – Hathor and Isis especially – were particularly concerned with women, of whom they were patronesses.

Two goddesses were not exclusively concerned with suitably 'feminine pursuits' but were associated with more intellectual concepts: Maat was the goddess of justice, truth and social order; Seshat was the goddess of writing and keeper of the royal annals. Maat's role is perhaps indicative of the fact that women were regarded as forces for stability; Seshat's is ironic considering that most ancient Egyptian women could not read or write.

Goddesses could have several seemingly conflicting aspects: Serket, for example, guarded the dead, but she also punished wrongdoers; Sekhmet had a fierce, warlike aspect, but she was also the patroness of doctors (see page 74), who used her weapons to drive out the demons that were thought to cause sickness.

The goddess Hathor, who was Isis's only real rival for the devotion of the Egyptians, also had two contrasting aspects. She, in the form of the fierce lioness-goddess, Sekhmet, was once dispatched by a disgruntled Re to destroy mankind. When Re changed his mind, she was only prevented from carrying out her mission by being tricked into drunkenness through drinking barley beer, dyed with red ochre to mislead her into thinking that it was blood. On the other hand Hathor was also the loving wife of Horus, searching him out after his eyes had been gouged out by Seth, healing him, and bearing him a son. She took an especial interest in women, providing husbands for young girls and protecting women in childbirth; and once entertained the sun god, Re, by lifting up her dress and letting him see her vagina!

Ancient Egyptian mythology gives many examples of the stereotype of the faithful female, but in some mythological stories a goddess is the protagonist, playing an active role. As we have seen above, Hathor is such a heroine. Another is Isis, who plays a major part in the mythological story of Osiris and was the role model for wives and mothers.

Isis was the sister and wife of Osiris, the divine king of Egypt who ruled beneficently for many years until he was murdered by his jealous brother, Seth. Seth sealed Osiris's body inside a wooden chest and threw it into the Nile, whence it was carried down to the sea, finally being cast up on the shore at Byblos (in Lebanon). There a great tamarisk tree grew up around the chest; and the king of Byblos, unaware of what the tamarisk concealed, cut down the tree to make it into the central pillar in the great hall of his palace. The grieving Isis, not knowing what had happened to her husband, set out to search for him and at last located and retrieved his body; and then made herself pregnant by him. Osiris was resurrected and made king of the Underworld, and Isis, having proved herself a devoted wife, was left alone to guard the child in her womb against Seth until it could be safely delivered. She was captured by Seth, who lusted after her, but escaped and took refuge in the Delta marshes until her son, Horus, was born; when the boy was fifteen years old, she brought him before the Tribunal of the Gods to claim his inheritance. She supported him throughout the eighty years that it took before Horus triumphed over his enemy, Seth, and gained the throne of Egypt.

Isis was the most popular goddess in Egypt, and was usually represented either as the faithful companion and protectress of Osiris or as the mother of Horus, seated with her son on her knee, suckling him. But Isis had another aspect: that of a wily, scheming woman who used her skills as a magician to gain her own ends. She used magic in her struggle against Seth to fulfil her ambitions for her son, Horus; and she used it against the great sun god, Re himself, in order to discover his secret name so that she would become his equal as a magician.

Hathor was a very ancient deity whose cult went back to predynastic times. Some of the columns in her great cult temple at Dendera, which have capitals in the form of the head of a woman with cow's ears, are a reminder that she was originally worshipped as a sacred cow in times when the Egyptians worshipped animals. The origins of Isis, on the other hand, are unknown. It is thought that originally she was worshipped in the Delta, and she may have been a personification of the throne of Egypt – her name means 'seat' or 'throne'. By the Late Period her cult had spread

Isis and Horus statue, Graeco-Roman Period

throughout Egypt and beyond, although it is curious that she had no major cult centre of her own in Egypt proper, but was allotted a space in or near the temples of other deities. The most famous of her temples is on the island of Philae, which is south of the First Cataract and, therefore, in Nubia.

Isis's role as ever-faithful wife and devoted mother gained her many adherents among women, and her reputation as a great magician appealed to the magic-conscious Egyptians of both sexes. Most of Isis's followers did not worship her in temples. Temples in ancient Egypt were not places of worship in the way that churches, mosques and synagogues are to us. They were places where the forces of chaos, which the Egyptians thought were a perennial threat to Egypt, were kept at bay by priests. Ordinary people never entered a temple; and the only direct contact they had with the gods was when the statues of the deities were carried in procession out of the temples on great festive occasions.

In spite of this, Isis was popular among those who could never dream of entering her temples. During the Late Period she became a universal goddess, assimilating with deities such as Hathor, Bastet, Nut, Sothis, Astarte and Renenutet; and, under first the Ptolemies and then the Romans, her cult spread beyond Egypt, finally arriving in Britain. She was the most popular deity in the Roman Empire, her only rival being Mithras. In the second century AD, Apuleius described her in *The Golden Ass*, where she addresses him thus:

> I am Nature, the universal Mother, mistress of all the elements, primordial child of time, sovereign of all things spiritual, queen of the dead, queen also of the immortals, the single manifestation of all gods and goddesses that are . . . Though I am worshipped in many aspects, known by countless names, and propitiated with all manner of different rites, yet the whole round earth venerates me . . . and the Egyptians who excel in ancient learning and worship me with ceremonies proper to my godhead, call me by my true name, namely, Queen Isis.[9]

The cult of Isis was superseded only by that of the Virgin Mary and the Infant Jesus, whose iconography seems to have been derived from ancient Egyptian depictions of Isis with her son, Horus, sitting on her knee. The image of mother and child is obviously one that both pagans and Christians have found potent; and it is probably Isis's image and reputation as a mother that explains a good deal of her great popularity. Above all, however, she, like the Virgin Mary, was a sympathetic figure: her own suffering as a bereaved wife and her travails on behalf of her son allowed her to understand the sorrows of her worshippers.

On the evidence of literary and artistic sources, it would seem that ancient Egyptian women were not valued for their intellect, although it was admitted, at least by men, that they had a capacity for cunning. The stereotypes range from goddess to scheming whore, with the favourite image of woman being that of devoted wife or doting mother. It is perhaps not surprising to learn that in their attitudes towards women, the ancient Egyptians were not so dissimilar from most other societies.

CHAPTER TWO

WOMEN IN SOCIETY: I

Social and Legal Position

In pharaonic Egypt women were accorded a relatively high social status. As in any country, at any period of time, mothers of families exercised a degree of authority in the home and commanded a special place in society at large; but women held none of the important offices of state and, apart from queens regnant and certain priestesses (see Chapter Eight), wielded very little political power. In spite of this, ancient Egyptian women in general were able to exert a certain amount of influence outside the domestic sphere. This was largely due to the fact that all landed property was passed down through the female line from mother to daughter. The reason for such a rule seems to have been based on the assumption that one can be certain only of who one's mother is – maternity is a matter of fact, paternity is a matter of opinion! Thus, an ancient Egyptian man usually described himself by giving his mother's name rather than his father's, as in: Ahmose, son of (the woman) Abana; Baba, son of (the woman) Reonet. A belief in matrilineal descent is also found in other cultures – Jews, for example, owe their Jewishness to their mothers, not to their fathers.

The rule seems to have been fairly strictly adhered to, and nowhere more so than in the royal family (see page 148). The ideal way in which a king inherited the throne was by marriage to the royal heiress, the eldest daughter of the queen; because of this, some of them married every royal heiress regardless of consanguinity. The tradition of the royal heiress also explains why, although Egyptian kings were pleased to accept foreign princesses as wives, Egyptian princesses were not sent to make marriages abroad – even the most tenuous claim to being a royal heiress must not be allowed to enable a foreign ruler to make a claim to the Egyptian throne.

Although descent and kinship were traced through the female line, ancient Egypt was by no means a matriarchy. The real power lay in the hands of men: they held the great offices of state, they made up the bureaucracy that governed the land. A man's social standing determined the nature of the burial he was accorded and thus his success in the Afterlife: a peasant was buried in a simple grave dug in the desert sand, a nobleman merited a substantial tomb. The nature of a woman's burial depended on the social standing of her husband or father, for an ancient Egyptian woman of the tomb-owning classes shared her husband's tomb or, if she were unmarried, was buried in the family tomb which belonged to her father. Normally, only queens could expect independent burials.

In pharaonic Egypt, property not only passed through the female line, but rights to that property often devolved on women. They could own and administer it independently, whether it consisted of land or of possessions. It is difficult to obtain detailed information on land tenure in pharaonic Egypt, but one document, the Wilbour Papyrus, which is the chief source for land tenure in the New Kingdom, gives a rental record for 1143 BC. It shows that herdsmen rented 381 *arouras* (an *aroura* was equal to 0.68 acres) of land, soldiers 236, stablemasters 119, priests 103, and 'citizenesses'[1] 190 *arouras*.[2] This compares favourably with the position of women today, when it has been estimated that they own less than one hundredth of the world's property.[3]

The economic independence that ownership and rights to property gave to the women of pharaonic Egypt, together with their legal status of being equal with men under the law (see page 27), ensured that they enjoyed a fair amount of social freedom. They went about freely, with faces unveiled, unlike the women of ancient Greece who not only were required to cover their heads in a seemly manner but who, by the laws of Solon, were not permitted to go out at night without a lighted torch carried before them, or to leave home carrying more than three garments; and who were guarded within the house by chaperones, and sometimes by eunuchs or old men.

Within the house, there was no purdah for Egyptian women. Although in larger houses certain rooms were designated 'women's quarters' (*ipt*), women were not expected to remain in them. This was in sharp contrast to the women of ancient Greece who were confined to the women's apartments (*gynaeceum*) of their houses. These were the rooms at greatest distance from the entrance hall, and were usually in the upper storey of the building; and a woman was often not allowed to pass from her own part of the house to another without permission.

The contrast between the women of Egypt and those of his own country struck Herodotus forcibly. As a Greek he would have been accustomed to women leading a much more proscribed life, both legally and socially, than that enjoyed by the Egyptian women whom he had observed during the visit he made to Egypt sometime around 450 BC. In ancient Athens, for example, women were citizens only for the purposes of marriage and procreation; otherwise, they had no independent status of their own. They were under the protection and control of a guardian (*kyrios*), usually the male head of the family, for the whole of their lives. Within the family, Greek women were expected to perform domestic duties, to stay at home and to be silent. According to the playwright, Menander, 'The loom is woman's work and not debate.' In the opinion of Herodotus, however,

> The Egyptians, in their manners and customs, seem to have reversed the ordinary practices of mankind. For instance, women attend market and are employed in trade, while men stay at home and do the weaving.[4]

Greek women who lived in Egypt during the Ptolemaic Period enjoyed a higher status than that of Greek women in their own country. An important reason for this was that Ptolemaic Egypt, unlike Classical Athens, was a monarchy in which queens regularly played a part in government and even in warfare; and women of all classes participated, as was the Egyptian tradition, in both domestic and public economy. It has been suggested[5] that perhaps Greek women observed Egyptian women and were encouraged to assert themselves. For example, under Greek law a woman needed the consent of her *kyrios* for financial transactions of more than a trivial value (i.e. an amount greater than the price of a *medimnus* of barley – a *medimnus* could sustain an average family for six days). In Ptolemaic Egypt a woman was given the option of acting under Egyptian rather than Greek law, in which case she was not required to have a *kyrios*. Greek women observing Egyptian women acting without *kyrioi* must have realized that all women were capable of doing so!

Many of the scenes of everyday life sculpted and painted on the walls of tombs illustrate the social freedom of ancient Egyptian women. Wives are depicted taking part with their husbands in their business activities – inspecting estates, at the cattle-count, watching craftsmen at work or labourers in the fields. Some women are depicted undertaking business of their own – a vignette in the tomb of Kenamun at Thebes, for example, shows an Eighteenth Dynasty woman merchant squatting behind her merchandise. In the New Kingdom it became fashionable to decorate tombs with scenes of feasting: the guests at the feasts are both male and female. In sporting scenes husbands are often accompanied by their wives and children, although, as we have seen in Chapter One, these scenes are often designed with erotic intent. As we shall see in the following pages business and legal documents, wills and letters often demonstrate the amount of social freedom enjoyed by women in ancient Egypt.

Social life as depicted on the walls of tombs was that led by the upper classes. The majority of Egyptians were peasants, and an ancient Egyptian peasant woman, like her modern sister, led a hard life of menial toil which was interrupted, but only briefly, at regular intervals for the incessant bearing of children. She aged very quickly and died comparatively young. Only if her son 'made good' (and this was possible in Egypt where a talented man could rise from lowly origins) and used his new-found wealth to make his family more comfortable, could she enjoy an easier life. Peasant women looked after their children, cleaned their houses, cooked for their families and washed clothes. Many of these domestic tasks were performed outside the house: cooking was often done out of doors; clothes were washed communally on the banks of canals or of the Nile; water had to be fetched from the river or from canals or wells – scenes of female domestic activity that can still be seen in the rural Egypt of today. Peasant women also helped in the fields, especially at harvest time when, as today, the whole family was involved in gathering in the harvest. Winnowing was usually women's work and young girls could be set to glean. Women, not men, went to market, and much farm produce was carried by them in baskets on their heads, or, as in the case of birds, in their hands.

Upper class women enjoyed an easier life. In their households, servants, who were often men, were employed. In earlier times the washing, spinning and weaving was undertaken by women, but in the New Kingdom men became launderers and weavers. The cooking in an upper class household was usually done by men although the worst task of all, the back-breaking daily job of grinding grain by hand on a stone saddle quern, was performed by female servants.

The fact that, unlike women of most ancient civilizations and also of some modern countries, ancient Egyptian women enjoyed the same rights under the law as ancient Egyptian men goes a long way towards explaining their relatively high social position. 'You have made a power for the women equal to that of the men', words written in praise of Isis and quoted in a papyrus of the second century AD,[6] might have been written with this in mind; and the point is one that many scholars have commented upon.[7] The *de jure* rights of an ancient Egyptian woman depended upon her class in society and not upon her sex. The King of Egypt was chief lawgiver and upholder of the law; and in theory everyone in Egypt, both male and female, noble and peasant, was equal under the law and had the right of access to the king in order to obtain justice. In practice, as might be expected, some, notably the rich and powerful, were more equal than others.

An Egyptian woman was legally *capax* and enjoyed full rights under the law. She was her own mistress and, whether she was married or not, could act on her own behalf without being obliged to have a guardian act for her.[8] As we shall see from examples quoted in the following pages, she could bring an action at law; she could act as a witness to legal documents and as an executrix of wills; she could adopt children in her own name and she could be a partner in legal contracts – for instance, she could sign her own marriage contract (see page 65). A woman could buy and sell: if a woman owned property she could dispose of it, whether it consisted of land or possessions, as she wished. In one papyrus a certain Sebtitis cedes to her daughter half an *aroura* (0.34 acres) of corn-land;[9] in another, several women acting together record a sale of land.[10]

It is clear from several papyri that sometimes a woman preferred to use an agent in such transactions. An example of this is found in a disputed case, from around 775 BC, of land purchase which was settled by appealing to the oracle of the god Hemen of Hefat:

> They began to dispute again today concerning the payment for the parcels of land belonging to the townswoman Ipip, which Paneferher, the son of her employee (?) Harsiesi, sold to Ikeni . . . Hemen said concerning the two written documents which were placed before him: 'Ikeni is right. He has handed over to Paneferher the money which reverted to the [woman Ipip] . . . It is paid.'[11]

There is just a suspicion, here, that Ipip's agent may have been trying to cheat her by claiming that Ikeni had not paid him the money owed on the land!

Evidence from papyri shows that even during the Ptolemaic Period, when Egypt was governed by Greeks, women acted in law according to Egyptian rather than Greek custom. In many of these papyri women, whose names indicate that they are Egyptian, are recorded as concluding bargains, stating accounts, making petitions, lending money, and even selling land; but some papyri record that even women of Greek origin could occasionally undertake such transactions on their own behalf. One such was Apollonia,[12] although since she was also called by an Egyptian name, Senmonthis, her lineage may have been Egyptian. Her history is an interesting one. She lived in Pathyris, 30 km south of Thebes (Luxor), in the second century BC; and was the daughter of a soldier, appropriately enough since her Egyptian name means 'sister of Montu (the god of war)'. The names of four generations of her paternal ancestors are known: except for her great-great-grandfather and several lesser relatives, all have both Greek and Egyptian names, like Apollonia/Senmonthis herself. They were reputed to be 'Cyrenean', and, if so, they may have arrived in Egypt from Cyrene at least a century before the birth of Apollonia. On the other hand, they may have been native Egyptians who were given a false ethnic origin upon entering the army, a common practice.

Around 150 BC, when Apollonia/Senmonthis was about twenty years old, she married a cavalry officer in his late forties named Dryton. He had been married before, and had a son by his first wife; he was destined to have five daughters with Apollonia, none of whom remotely rivalled his son in Dryton's affection.[13] As soon as he married for the second time, Dryton made the first of the four wills that he eventually drew up: in this will he names Apollonia, his son and any children that he and Apollonia may have as beneficiaries. Twenty-four years later, in the last of his wills, his dispositions ignore Apollonia:

> As to my wife Apollonia also called Senmonthis, if she stays at home and is irreproachable, they shall give every month for four years for the maintenance of herself and her two daughters two and a half *artaba*[14] of wheat, one twelfth of croton [for oil] and 200 copper drachmas.[15]

Why Dryton chose to treat his wife so shabbily, leaving nothing to her but maintenance for herself and their two youngest daughters for four years; and making even this income provisional upon the judgement of her stepson and daughters as to her irreproachability, we do not know. He does, however, concede that 'whatever property Senmonthis may have evidently acquired for herself while married to Dryton, she is to continue to own.'[16]

Fortunately for Apollonia/Senmonthis, she was a woman of property, some of which she had inherited from her father – a quarter-share of 35 *arouras* of land, the other three quarters being left equally to her three sisters.[17] Eight and three quarters of an *aroura* was considered to be a large holding for a woman. In 135 BC, she and her three sisters were forced to take legal action against their great-uncle and his two sons, who had seized the property because Apollonia's father had not been precise enough in his will.[18] Apollonia's daughters were eventually to encounter the same problem, having to bring an action at law against a certain Ariston from Thebes, who had taken possession of the land that their father had left them near Thebes because 'he knew that we were women and lived in another place.'[19]

Apollonia was a considerable lender of property, usually acting for herself in the transactions although on three occasions Dryton acted as *kyrios* (see page 31), perhaps because he was at home and insisting that his wife act according to Greek law. Other documents record that in 136 BC she leased 35 *arouras* of land belonging to a temple of Hathor;[20] that she loaned grain to a veteran;[21] that she loaned 1 talent and 5,030 copper drachmas;[22] that she loaned 1 talent and 4,000 drachmas.[23] She seems to have made money on her transactions.

The Greeks were horrified that Egyptian women could own land and were considered *capax* at law. In one papyrus,[24] two women make a claim to be reinstated in the possession of property inherited by them from their father. It is clear that the property had devolved on the daughters as the natural heirs-at-law but that their nearest male relative, apparently taking advantage of the introduction into Egypt of Greek ideas, had seized possession of it. It is interesting to note that the papyrus records that the women had paid the succession duties (*fiscus*) on the property not, as might be expected, to the king but to the queen. As a concession to the scruples of his Greek subjects on the necessity for a woman to act under the guidance of a *kyrios*, the unpopular Ptolemy Philopator (221–205 BC) decreed that the names of a husband or male relative should be added to documents as a woman's legal guardian in transacting business.[25]

Apollonia/Senmonthis was affected by this decree, which remained in force long after Philopator's death: one papyrus records that she had loaned wheat without interest to Apollonius and his wife, Herais;[26] another that she had loaned money to

Nechoutes;[27] and a third that she had loaned money to Saeis and Harmais.[28] In all three papyri, Apollonia acts with her husband, Dryton, as guardian.

A married woman in ancient Egypt had the same rights to own, inherit and dispose of property as one who was unmarried; her property did not automatically pass into the hands of her husband on marriage, a state of affairs not matched in modern England until the Married Women's Property Act of 1882. A married woman had the right to protect her own property, and when engaged in a lawsuit was considered to be a completely independent legal personality, as in the papyrus quoted below, which dates to about 1786 BC, in which it is a married woman who is recorded as plaintiff and not her husband:

> My father has committed an irregularity. He had in his posses-
> sion certain objects belonging to me which my husband had
> given me. But he (my father) made them over to his second wife,
> Senebtisi. May I obtain restitution thereof.[29]

A married woman's rights to her own property extended to her ability to make a loan to her own husband, as for instance, in the case of a woman named Tay-hetem who, in 249 BC, loaned her husband 3 *deben* of silver (273 grammes) at 30 per cent interest, to be paid back within three years as was usual.[30]

There were several ways in which a woman could acquire property. One, of course, was by purchase;[31] another in payment for work done;[32] a third by inheritance from parents, brothers and, in the case of married women, from husbands.[33] Normal legal conditions decreed that a wife was entitled to one third of her husband's property after his death, with the other two thirds being divided between her husband's children (note, not hers by a previous marriage) and his brothers and sisters: a disposition not dissimilar to the situation among Muslims in Egypt today. Normally, in return for her inheritance of her husband's property, an ancient Egyptian woman was required to undertake the care of his tomb. Contracts have been found in which a wife is bound to bury her husband and maintain his tomb.[34]

If a husband wished his wife to inherit more than the third of his property to which she would normally be entitled, it was possible for him to take steps before his death to donate property to her. For example, in one Middle Kingdom will a husband left fifteen slaves, one third of whom his wife inherited as her normal share. Another sixty slaves are mentioned in the will. These slaves, however, had been given to the wife during her husband's lifetime, thus becoming her own property and therefore not subject to disposal in her husband's will. It is perhaps worth commenting here on the vexed question of slavery in pharaonic Egypt. Some authorities have doubted that such an institution existed in ancient Egypt, where, as we have seen (page 27), everyone was equal under the law. However, certain categories of people could be the property of others, who could buy, sell, rent or bequeath them, although even these 'slaves' had possessions and servants of their own, and owned and inherited land, which they could dispose of as they wished. They often married free women. In a discussion of serfs and slaves,[35] it has been noted that there were individuals, at least in the Late Period, who were so 'unfree' that they can only be called slaves, but this is perhaps an indication of foreign customs prevailing in Egypt.

The laws of inheritance could be circumvented in ways other than the one outlined above. In a famous case in the Twentieth Dynasty, adoption was resorted to, the adoption document stating:

> Nebnefer, my husband, made a writing for me, the chantress of Seth, Nenefer, making me a child of his and writing down to me all he possessed, having no son or daughter apart from myself.[36]

The object of Nebnefer's adoption of his own wife was to prevent his brothers and sisters 'rising up to confront her . . . saying "Let my brother's portion be given to me".' The adoption document was witnessed by 'many witnesses' including several women – Adjedaa, the wife of one of the male witnesses; the chantress of Seth, Taiuhery; and the chantress of Anty, Tanetnephthys.

The normal inheritance law whereby two thirds of property were inherited by children, brothers and sisters, applied only to male testators. A woman, being free under the law to dispose of her own property as she wished, was perfectly entitled to disinherit her children if she so desired. This is what Naunakhte did in the New Kingdom, testifying before a tribunal:

> But see, I am grown old. And see, they [her children] are not looking after me in my turn. Whosoever of them has aided me, to him shall I give of my property. [37]

She then listed her eight children by name, noting what, if anything, each was to inherit.

Sometimes, the disposal of property extended to the disposal of the woman herself – in other words, self-enslavement. This was forbidden but, nevertheless, sometimes occurred for a variety of reasons. For example, one woman who owed money but was unable to repay her creditor sold herself to him 'to do what he wished by day and by night'. Another woman, in 137 BC, sold herself to a temple for ninety-nine years. Such a long period of time meant that her children and grandchildren were also committed by the transaction, and would presumably fall into the category of the 'unfree'. In addition this woman also paid a fee of one and a quarter *kite* (approximately 11 grammes) of copper per month. In return for all this, she expected the god of the temple to look after her:

> You shall protect me, you shall keep me safe, you shall keep me sound, you shall protect me from every demon . . .

The equality of women with men, both before the law and in ownership of property, is well illustrated by a lawsuit brought by a scribe of the treasury of the Temple of Ptah in Memphis, a man named Mose.[38] The proceedings of the trial, which took place during the reign of Ramesses II (1304–1238 BC), are recorded on a wall of Mose's tomb at Sakkara. The subject of the litigation was ownership of a piece of land near Memphis which, according to Mose, had been given to an ancestor of his, Neshi, a ship's captain, by King Ahmose in about 1550 BC. Some three hundred years later, a descendant of Captain Neshi, a woman named Wernero, was appointed by the court to cultivate the land as a trustee for her five sisters and brothers. One of the sisters, however, objected to this, and a new order was made dividing the land between the six heirs. Wernero and her son, Huy, appealed against the decision, but unfortunately Huy died at this point, and when his widow, Nebnofret, began to cultivate his share of the land, she was forcibly ejected from it by a man named Kha'y, who was presumably a relative.

In 1322 BC, Nebnofret brought a court action against Kha'y but the findings went against her. Several years later, her son, Mose, tried to have the ruling reversed. When the title-deeds were examined, it became obvious that there had been some forgery, and Nebnofret suggested that the official records should be consulted by Kha'y and a court official, a proposal which led to Kha'y and the official colluding in the expunging of Huy's name from the records. Judgement was therefore given in favour of Kha'y, and Mose was forced to establish the fact that he was indeed descended from Captain Neshi; that his father had cultivated the land and had paid taxes on it over the years. He did so with the help of sworn witnesses, both men and women, and, although the final part of the hieroglyphic inscription is lost, it seems safe to assume that Mose regained his inheritance.

One of the most interesting aspects of Mose's lawsuit is the confirmation it gives that women could own land, could act as trustees, could initiate court actions and be held to be as competent in a law court as men, all aspects of the equality under the law that they enjoyed. The advantages that this equality gave to the women of ancient Egypt cannot be overestimated, for their legal status had such a profound effect on their lives.

CHAPTER THREE

WOMEN IN SOCIETY: II

Female Occupations and Professions

The majority of Egyptians, both male and female, were illiterate. How many of either sex could read and write is impossible to establish, but it is certain that, in common with all traditional societies, women were less literate than men. A relatively small proportion of ancient Egyptian society was employed in the bureaucracy or as artisans and craftsmen; by far the largest was engaged in agricultural work. Thus, it follows that the majority of ancient Egyptian women were uneducated peasants. The ancient Egyptians might not have subscribed to the notion that a woman's place is wholly in the home, but neither, it seems, did they consider it desirable that many women should receive the formal education (see page 124) that would fit them to have a career outside the home, either in the civil service or as holders of public office; or be trained for employment as artisans and craftsmen. No woman, as far as we know, was ever engaged as a stonemason or quarryman, although perhaps they would not have considered this to be a matter of regret.

Reliefs in tombs, and the servant statues and models that were placed in the tomb to work for the deceased in the Afterlife,[1] provide ample evidence that women were largely engaged in indoor domestic activities such as the preparation of food and cleaning in their own houses; or undertaking the same occupations as servants in the households of others, where they were employed in the kitchen, cooking, baking bread and brewing beer; or as servants waiting on guests at banquets. In all of these occupations, they worked alongside men. The main activity for peasant women, beyond their own homes, was going to market; and, as in many

Servants: relief from *mastaba*-tomb of Mereruka, Sakkara, Sixth
Dynasty

Third World countries today, they must have spent a great deal of
time collecting fuel and drawing and carrying water. Butchery,
vinery and outdoor activities such as herding cattle, calving and
milking seem to have been the exclusive province of men. The
heavy work in the fields – ploughing, hoeing and cutting the wheat
or barley – was done by men; women helped with the weeding and
at harvest time. This is consistent with women's practice at other
times and in other places where, as in ancient Egypt, cultivation of
the land is intense, necessitating the use of short-fallow and
ploughing techniques.[2]

Women did not play a large part in public life. This was largely because civil status was usually patrilineal: a man was often able to hand on his office, but he did so to his son rather than to his daughter. One example of this, dating from the Twelfth Dynasty, is the deed of transfer which a man named Mery, son of Inyotef, drew up in favour of his son, Iuseneb:

> I transfer my office of *phylarch* to my son, Iuseneb, on condition that he is a support for me in my old age, because I have grown infirm. Let him be appointed to it immediately.

Mery went on in the deed to say:

> As for the conveyance which I drew up previously in favour of his mother, it is revoked; and as for my house situated in the region of Hatmadet – it is for the children who may be borne to me by Satnebet-nen-in-esu.[3]

So it seems that not only was his wife to lose her share of his property, but that he had taken a new wife to boot.

A second important reason for sons rather than daughters appearing in public life was that it was sons who were nearly always the executors of mortuary offerings. If a daughter married, she was expected to move away from home to live with her husband, but a son, even if married, was more likely to remain on the property that he had inherited from his father, and thus be on hand to make the funerary offerings at the paternal tomb. Women were sometimes employed as mortuary priests[4] but perhaps only in cases where there was no son to undertake the task.

Although as a rule women did not hold public office, there is evidence from titles held by women in the Middle Kingdom[5] that, in this period at least, some women in the private sector held positions of trust such as treasurer and major-doma. There are several recorded instances of women holding supervisory positions such as superintendent of the dining-hall; overseer of the wig-shop; overseer of singers; overseer of amusements; mistress of the royal harem; and overseer of the house of weavers.

The textile industry seems to have been dominated by women, both as workers and as supervisors. Women are seen at work in, for example, the wooden model of a weaving workshop from the Eleventh Dynasty tomb of Meketre at Deir el-Bahri; and in reliefs in several of the Twelfth Dynasty nobles' tombs at Beni Hasan (Pl. 5). Roving and spinning seem to have been female specialities.[6] In the New Kingdom, several women were overseers of weavers on the estates of the Temple of Amun at Karnak;[7] and in the royal residence established in that period at Gurob in the Faiyum,[8] the manufacture of cloth as a state industry was a particular concern of the royal harem. The ladies of the harem were responsible for the training and supervision of textile workers and, it has been suggested,[9] even undertook some of the more delicate work themselves to occupy their time.

Apart from the occupations that were deemed to be largely the province of women, there were five professions open to them – priesthood, midwifery, mourning, dancing and music – of which the most prestigious was priesthood. Little is known about what sort of training was undertaken by women choosing careers in these professions, although women with an aptitude for dancing and the playing of musical instruments must have had some, especially if they wished to develop their talent to professional standards. As for 'the oldest profession in the world' – prostitution – there is very little actual evidence of it in ancient Egypt, although from literary sources there are references to *hnmwt* – professional singers or dancers – who were not averse to bestowing sexual favours for payment.[10] Documents from the workmen's village at Deir el-Medina refer to women who are not wives but belong to 'the others', perhaps meaning prostitutes; and the erotic papyrus now in the Turin Museum (see page 7), which is a notable exception to the convention that ancient Egyptian texts and representations of sexual activity should be very discreet, depicts, in a very frank way, the erotic antics of what can only be one or more prostitutes.[11]

Of the five female professions, the priesthood conferred the highest professional status upon women. Religion played an important part in ancient Egyptian life and it was by active participation in religious affairs that a woman enhanced her social standing. As early as the Fourth Dynasty women were allowed to participate in religious life by attending on deities as priestesses in temples, especially those belonging to female deities such as Hathor and Neith, although they could also be in the service of gods. For many centuries members of the lowest social classes, be they male or female, were excluded from these positions, but, by the New Kingdom, women of all classes were allowed to seek employment in temple service, and very many of them did so. Some were married, others not. Some came from the upper class families which would normally supply part-time members of the male priesthood, others known to have been priestesses were wives or daughters of artists, weavers or shoemakers,[12] in other words, members of artisan families which had no hereditary connections with temples. Women participated in a cult for both religious and social reasons: the holding of a priestly title carried a certain amount of prestige; it was taken as an indication that the holder was a woman of respectability and standing in society, and perhaps as an indication of her intellectual capabilities.

Unlike, for example, a Christian church or cathedral, an ancient Egyptian temple was not a place in which a god was worshipped by a congregation led by a spiritual leader who was also a preacher and instructor of his parishioners. Instead, it was considered to be the 'house of the god' (*ḥwt or pr nṯr*) from which the general public was excluded and in which the high priest performed his duties as 'servant of the god' (*ḥm nṯr*). The priests of the temple, called *w'bw* (meaning, '(ritually) pure ones') were administrators, specialists such as scribes or astronomers, and clergy who enacted the temple rituals – the morning service, for example, which was in essence giving the god his breakfast after washing and dressing him; or the evening service in which the god was given his supper and prepared for his night's rest. Most priests were part-time; the permanent officials of a temple were usually the 'superintendent of the temple' and the 'chief lector'; with minor officials such as door-keepers and floor-sweepers. The superintendent was usually the high priest himself and he often held the position of lector as well. In some large temples, the high priest wielded a great deal of temporal political power.[13]

Priestesses, in general, were neither administrators nor specialists, and wielded little influence outside the temple. They did, however, play a not inconsiderable part in the worship of temple divinities. One of their most important functions was to act as impersonators of goddesses. When the priestesses of Hathor danced in her honour they consciously imitated the graciousness for which the goddess was famed;[14] and in funerary ceremonies two female mourners impersonated Isis and Nephthys and were called the 'great kite' and the 'little kite', in commemoration of the fact that the two goddesses had assumed the form of these birds when they set out to find the body of the murdered Osiris.[15] Priestesses took part in the cult of the dead, which in many respects resembled that of the gods. One of the most important officiants in the mortuary cult was the *Ka*-servant (*ḥm-k3*), whose task was to perform the same services in the tomb-chapel as were performed in the temple by the *ḥm-nṯr*. On the evidence of the feminine determinatives found in the large body of inscriptions recorded in the *Urkunden* compiled by Sethe,[16] in the Old Kingdom at least, women could be *Ka*-servants.

Every temple seems to have had a number of priestesses attached to it as musician priestesses or chantresses. In the Middle Kingdom they were called *ḥnwt* (or *ḥnyt*) and from the New Kingdom onwards they were usually called *šmʿwt*: both words mean 'female musician'. They clapped their hands rhythmically and chanted 'he comes who brings, he comes who brings [happiness, good fortune etc.]' to welcome the king whenever he entered a temple. They sang hymns and played instruments such as harps and tambourines during temple services; they clicked their fingers or beat clappers[17] made of wood or bone; and they shook large bead necklaces, called *menit*, or rattled *sistra*. A *sistrum* was formed from a strip of metal bent into a loop, the ends of which were bound into a handle. Rods, usually three, were passed from one side of the loop to the other and threaded with metal beads, or left loose in their sockets, so that they rattled when the *sistrum* was shaken. At festivals priestesses danced through the streets, shaking their *menit*-necklaces and rattling their *sistra*, bestowing life, stability, health and happiness on the population in the name of the deity of their temple.

Meryt, wife of Sennefer, holding a *sistrum*; from tomb of Sennefer,
Thebes, Eighteenth Dynasty

In the New Kingdom, so many women are on record as musicians
of one god or another that it almost seems as though every female in
the land, from the highest to the lowest, took part in a cult.[18] The
inevitable consequence of such a widespread participation was a
lessening of the status of female priests. In contrast, the male
priesthood by this time had become largely professional and
hereditary, dominated by the men of a priestly class jealous of its
rank and the privileges that went with it. This state of affairs
contrasts sharply with the position of women during the Old

Menit-necklace found at Malkata Palace, Thebes

Kingdom in the cult of Hathor, in whose temples – the chief of
which were at Dendera, Sakkara and Cusae – women were not
employed exclusively as musicians. There were several priestly
titles used in the cult: *rḫt-nsw* (king's acquaintance), *ḫkrt-nsw-w'tt*
(sole royal concubine) and *w'bt Ḥwt-ḥr* (pure one of Hathor). None
of them was hereditary[19] and a woman could be a priestess in more
than one temple.[20] In the Hathor cult during the Old Kingdom, a
priestess, who bore the title *mrt*, was in charge of the management
of the estates of the goddess; and the high priest was sometimes a
woman (*ḥmt nṯr*).

In the Old and Middle Kingdoms, women of upper class families were regularly appointed high priestesses, most often of Hathor but they were also found in the same capacity in temples of Neith; and at Beni Hasan, the wives of the nobles who owned the tombs there were high priestesses of the local goddess, Pakhet.[21] In the Old Kingdom, one woman, Queen Meresankh, was high priestess of a god, Thoth.[22] In the Fifth Dynasty the sons and the daughter of one noble took it in turns to serve as high priest of Hathor[23] and apparently the woman exercised the function in exactly the same way as the men.

In the New Kingdom, the wife of the High Priest of Amun at Thebes was appointed 'Chief Concubine of Amen-Re'.[24] Her duties were to supervise and lead the female musicians of the temple (*šm'wt n 'Imn* – musicians of Amun), who in theory formed the god's 'harem', and who were attached to the Chief Concubine's household;[25] and to ensure the smooth functioning of temple life. As far as we know, the title concubine is not to be taken literally and the position held no sexual responsibilities. In the Twenty-first Dynasty the High Priestess of Amun at Thebes was known as 'The Divine Wife of Amun', 'The Adorer of the God' and 'The Hand of the God', and, as we shall see in Chapter Eight, held a position of great power and influence.

Like priests, priestesses were divided into four groups, called *s3* (*phyle* in Greek), each on duty for one month out of four. The leader of a *s3* of priestesses was called 'the great one of the musicians', and she was usually the wife of an important man, with whom she continued to live as normal. Although men were required to be celebate during their month of priestly duties, it seems that priestesses were not placed under the same obligation.

In ancient Egypt, midwifery was a recognized profession. Midwives are referred to in the Old Testament (Exodus, i, 16) where it was the midwives who were ordered to kill the first born. There was a school of midwifery in the Temple of Neith at Sais, in which women were trained by the temple staff, although it is probable that at a number of other temples, where Egyptian (male) doctors received their general medical training, gynaecological matters were considered to be a male province.

The esteem in which midwives were held is perhaps best

illustrated by a popular story in which it was clearly not considered to be beneath the dignity of goddesses to undertake the task of delivering babies. The story is in the Westcar Papyrus,[26] and tells of how the goddesses Isis, Nephthys, Meskhenet and Heket, disguised as musicians, were sent by the sun god, Re, to deliver the three children that he had fathered on Reddjedet, the wife of one of his priests at Heliopolis. During Reddjedet's labour she was supported by Isis and Nephthys; and Meskhenet, the goddess of fate who was also the personification of the birth-stool, stood by to predict the future for the children. Heket, the royal midwife, delivered the three sons of Reddjedet who were destined to become kings of Egypt.

Medicine in ancient Egypt was relatively advanced and Egyptian doctors, who were all, with one or two exceptions, male, were skilled (see page 74). But they specialized in female diseases rather than obstetrics, and the delivery of babies was usually left to women. Thus female relatives and friends would attend a woman in childbirth, assisted by the local midwife. The majority of ancient Egyptian midwives were untrained, and such skills as they had would have been acquired through experience. Nevertheless, there must have been midwives without any professional training who had earned good reputations; and these women would presumably have been in great demand.

Mothers often died in childbirth (see page 84) or were unable to nurse their children, necessitating in the use of a wet-nurse – a custom that was especially prevalent, for social rather than medical reasons, in the upper classes. Thus, many poor women who either had more than enough milk for their own child's needs, or whose own child had died, were able to hire themselves out as wet-nurses. The work of a wet-nurse was undertaken on a professional basis and there are several examples of contracts negotiated between wet-nurses and their employers. In one of them, dating to 233/231 BC, a woman named Sponnesis agreed to be wet-nurse for three years to an Egyptian baby boy, providing milk from both breasts, in return for which she was promised a salary of 350 drachma, oil and her board.[27]

Wet-nurses naturally exerted a great influence on the children they nursed, a factor that was especially significant in royal circles, of course. In the New Kingdom, a number of high officials found it politically expedient to marry royal wet-nurses.[28] In their tombs, they took pains to record the fact: Amenemhab, for example, lieutenant-commander of soldiers during the reigns of Tuthmosis III and Amenhotep II, and owner of Tomb No. 85 at Thebes, whose wife is depicted with a young prince at her breast; and Kenamun (Tomb No. 93), whose wife is shown in his tomb nursing the young king, Amenhotep II.

A career in mourning[29] was followed by many ancient Egyptian women. Those who could afford it employed professional mourners to grieve openly about the house while the dead man was being mummified, a process which took seventy days; and to follow the funeral cortège to the tomb. The mourning took the form of casting dust on the head, rending clothes and scratching cheeks while wailing. Judging from tomb-paintings, the profession of mourner could start at an early age: in the tomb of Ramose at Thebes, for

Widow casting dust on head, tomb of Nebamun and Ipuky, Thebes, Eighteenth Dynasty

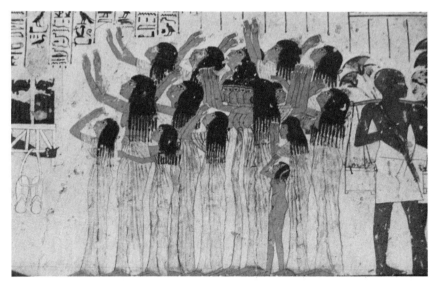

Mourners, from tomb of Ramose, Thebes, Eighteenth Dynasty

example, a group of mourning women has in its midst a very young girl. All are standing with upraised arms and obviously shrieking as loudly as they can – just as women in Egypt mourn today.

A suitably gifted woman could choose an honourable career in dancing. The Romans considered that dancing was unworthy of a man of rank: in Cicero's opinion, no man who was sober or in his right mind danced, either in company or when he was alone, for dancing signified loose behaviour and dissoluteness. For the ancient Egyptians, however, dancing was an accepted part of life, much as it was in Greece. In ancient Egypt, dancing was part of religious ritual before it also became secular, and women as well as men performed both kinds of dance. The Dance of the Muu,[30] for example, was a very ancient ceremony enacted at funerals by male dancers wearing strange tall reed head-dresses. Festivals such as the Sed or Jubilee, the Raising of the Djed Pillar, Opet and the Processions of Sacred Barques were all accompanied by dancers. Even the king sometimes danced: in the Temple of Hathor at Dendera, for instance, where he was greeted by the chant: 'The King comes to dance, he comes to sing. Sovereign Lady, see how he dances; Wife of Horus, look how he leaps.'

The pleasure-loving ancient Egyptians loved to dance; to them, it was a natural expression of joy. When the harvest was gathered in, farmers danced to give thanks to god; and no private party or feast was complete without dancing. Secular dances appear in the reliefs on the walls of Old Kingdom tombs, making it obvious that, during the life of the tomb-owner, they had been provided as entertainments at banquets and parties, a custom that continued into the New Kingdom. Inscriptions accompanying some reliefs inform us that there were also professional dancers whose services could be hired. Otherwise, amateurs danced to entertain the company; and it was perfectly proper for a man to call upon the women of his household to dance for his guests.

Given the enjoyment that ancient Egyptians derived from dancing, both as spectators and as participants, it is not surprising that women with a talent for dancing should take it up as a profession. Nothing is known of the kind or extent of the training that professional dancers of either sex received, but judging from reliefs, girls began dancing professionally in early childhood: some reliefs depict female dancers so young that they are shown naked. No choreographic notation has survived – indeed, it is unlikely that there was one – and so dance steps can only be reconstructed from reliefs. The Swiss Egyptologist, Henri Wild, studied dancing scenes and recognized steps and positions such as running, leaping, pirouetting; arm and hip movements while the feet remain still; walking on the toes; arms curved above the head.

Some dances involved the use of balls: in the Middle Kingdom tombs at Beni Hasan, women are depicted dancing and throwing and catching balls in positions that seem to be more appropriate to juggling; and some Old Kingdom reliefs show women with balls attached to the ends of their long plaits which they are swinging from side to side or brushing along the ground as they bend over. Other dances involved the use of mirrors.[31] In these, a dancer held a mirror in one hand and used it to reflect her other hand, or a hand-shaped object: this type of dance seems to have been associated with Hathor. In the New Kingdom, female dancers are depicted with castanets or tambourines in their hand, bending their bodies in sinuous movements not unlike those of native Egyptian

Acrobatic dancers on quartzite block from Karnak, during the time
of Hatshepsut, Eighteenth Dynasty

Acrobatic dancer, Deir el-Medina

dancers today; and, in this period especially, acrobatic dancing seems to have been fashionable, as evidenced in reliefs showing girls somersaulting or bending over backwards. At the same time, a more erotic type of dance came into vogue, performed by girls wearing nothing but a thong around their hips, which was sewn with hollow beads containing little stones that tinkled seductively as the girls swayed their hips.

A career in music was open to ancient Egyptian women. It is clear from reliefs in tombs and temples that throughout their history the ancient Egyptians regarded music both as a proper accompaniment to religious ceremonies and as something to be listened to and enjoyed. They often made their own music with simple instruments such as rattles[32] made of clay or plaited reed or straw, often shaped like gourds and filled with pebbles or beads, and drums; and, just like their counterparts today, sang and chanted as they worked. There were, however, professional musicians who played a variety of instruments; and judging from the story in the Westcar Papyrus[33] in which a group of female deities chose to disguise themselves as travelling musicians, such itinerant bands were not so uncommon as to excite attention. Every large household had a group of its own musicians, some of whom played instruments while others 'sang' – this singing is probably better termed chanting. A good example of such a group is the model found in the tomb of Katenen at Sakkara, in which Katenen and his wife are shown being entertained by two harpists and three female singers. The profession of musician was open to both men and women, although in the New Kingdom in particular, female musicians seem to have been in fashion.

We cannot know what ancient Egyptian music sounded like, but instruments have survived and by studying these and representations of them in reliefs, attempts – not entirely successful – have been made to reconstruct the stringing and fingering of stringed instruments and to discover the scales used. Rhythm seems to have played an essential part, and this was provided by drums, tambourines, clappers (castanets), *sistra* and *menit*-necklaces (see page 40); and by clapping hands and clicking fingers.

The earliest musical instruments were flutes[34] and harps[35] which, at first, were used only to accompany singers; both types of instrument were played by female as well as male musicians. The oldest type of flute, attested in Egypt from as early as the predynastic period, was the kind that is held downwards at an oblique angle when played – the so-called end-flute. An end-flute could be up to a metre or so long, made of reed, wood or metal, and usually had between four and six holes, with the longest examples having eight. The ancient Egyptians had other wind instruments in the shape of single-reed pipes (clarinet-type), which date back to at least the Fifth Dynasty, and double-reed pipes (oboe-type), the earliest of which dates to the New Kingdom.

There were two types of harp, the arched or bow-shaped and the angular. The bow-shaped harp came into use at least as early as the Fourth Dynasty, although the angular harp seems to have been imported into Egypt from Asia Minor at a much later date. Harps varied considerably in size, ranging from small, hand-held instruments to harps taller than the person standing to play them. The number of strings was not fixed, ranging from four to, on the largest instruments, ten or more; and although they were fixed to pegs at the upper end of the harp, the pegs do not seem to have been tightened for tuning purposes. It is thought that tuning was done by untying the strings from their pegs and winding them round the neck of the harp.[36] Most harps were made of wood, although the finest bow-shaped harp in the British Museum's collection is made of wood, bone and faience. This harp, however, was a model and never meant to be played. There is no example of an angular harp in the British Museum collections, but there is a wooden statuette, probably dating from the Nineteenth Dynasty, depicting such an instrument played by a young woman.

Some time during the sixteenth or seventeenth century BC the lyre was introduced into Egypt. The earliest representation of this instrument is in a relief in the tomb of Khnumhotep at Beni Hasan, where it is in the hands of an Asiatic beduin; but later representations are few, which perhaps indicates that it was never a popular instrument. Lutes, on the other hand, which are not known in Egypt before the New Kingdom, became very popular. They were of two types: one in which the neck and soundbox were made of wood; and

Lute player, faience bowl, Twentieth Dynasty

another, smaller type in which the neck was wooden but the soundbox was of tortoise-shell. The neck of an Egyptian lute seems to have been fretted.[37] An instrument had two, sometimes three, strings, which were affixed to the top end of the neck by tassels in the manner shown in a pottery cosmetic vase from the New Kingdom, now in the British Museum, which has been shaped in the form of a woman playing a lute (Pl. 1).

Combinations of musicians are frequently depicted in tomb-reliefs from the Old Kingdom onwards. One such is from the tomb of Werirenptah at Sakkara, which dates to either the Fifth or Sixth Dynasty, and which is now in the British Museum. This relief is in two registers: the top shows a group of male musicians, two of whom are singing and beating time with their hands; each of the singers faces an instrumentalist, who is presumably accompanying him, one with an end-flute, the other with a bow-shaped harp. The lower register depicts four female dancers facing two female singers who are clapping their hands.

In the New Kingdom, judging by tomb-reliefs, male musicians were less popular than female, with the exception of male harpers, often blind, who entertained the company with songs exhorting their audience to live for the day, for no man can tell what will happen on the morrow. In many reliefs of the period, women are shown playing a variety of instruments, often as the orchestra for dancers. Their instruments are flutes and lutes; and harps, which range from small instruments held in the hand, to medium harps at which the musician kneels or squats to play, to large harps that are played standing up.

Two scenes from the Eighteenth Dynasty Theban tomb of Nebamun show female musicians at work. One scene depicts four

Musicians, tomb of Nakht, Thebes, Eighteenth Dynasty

female musicians accompanying two female dancers: three of the women are supplying the rhythm, two by clapping their hands, one by beating her hand on her knee, while the fourth is playing a double pipe of the oboe-type. The three non-instrumentalists are singing a song, the verse of which is written in hieroglyphs above their heads. Part of it reads as follows:

[Sweetly] smelling [flowers], given by Ptah and made by Geb.
His beauty is in every body.
Ptah has done this with his own hands . . .
The earth overflows with love of him.

The other relief from the tomb of Nebamun shows five female musicians. One is clapping, one is playing the double pipe, one a lute of the type that has a wooden soundbox, and one a lute with a tortoise-shell soundbox. The fifth is playing a rectangular tambour-ine,[38] an instrument that was very popular in the New Kingdom, and which was always played by a woman.

Most secular music was performed by professionals, for there is no record of any person of rank playing a musical instrument in public. There is, however, the famous relief from the tomb of Mereruka at Sakkara in which Mereruka is shown sitting at one end of a bed while his wife is seated opposite him playing a harp – an early example of (bed)chamber music! Professional musicians of either sex were esteemed. In many cultures female musicians and dancers were classed as prostitutes but in ancient Egypt they enjoyed a high status; and, as the story of Reddjedet shows (see page 44), the role was not considered to be beneath the dignity even of goddesses.

No matter how successful a woman was in the female priesthood, or as a midwife, mourner, dancer or musician, it is a depressing thought that these female professions were not as important or influential as those in the civil and public service, none of which was open to women. As far as a woman's professional ambitions were concerned, it is an uncomfortable fact that no woman could aspire to be a king's scribe, an army general, a governor of a city or a province, or an ambassador to foreign lands – the scope of her ambitions was strictly limited to those professions deemed suitable for women.

CHAPTER FOUR

LOVE AND MARRIAGE

Judging by the numbers of love poems in ancient Egyptian literature, that emotion played an important part in the lives of Egyptians of both sexes. In ancient Egypt a woman, not being kept in seclusion from men, had opportunities for meeting members of the opposite sex and falling in love. Unrequited love must have been as common there as elsewhere; and resorting to love potions, charms and spells to win the affection of a loved one was an option, given the ancient Egyptians' firm belief in magic.[1] Magic was also something a jealous woman had recourse to: 'To make the hair of a rival fall out – anoint her head with burnt lotus leaves boiled in *ben*-oil.'[2]

Love poems (see also page 9 foll.) often acknowledge that the power of love was felt by men and women alike. Take, for example, the feelings of the woman in love in the following poem:

> My heart beats rapidly
> When I think of my love for you.
> It does not allow me to act sensibly
> But jumps from its place.
> It does not allow me to put on a dress,
> Or to drape myself with my shawl.
> I put on no eyepaint,
> Nor do I anoint myself at all.
> 'Don't wait, go there,' it says to me,
> As often as I think of him.
> Don't act the fool, my heart,
> Why do you flutter?
> Be still until my brother comes to you.
> Many eyes will come as well,

So don't let people say about me,
'A woman distraught with love!'
But be still when you think of him.
My heart, don't beat so rapidly!

A man, also, was often distracted by love:

The voice of the wild goose cries out
When it is caught by the bait.
My love of you ensnares me,
I cannot free myself.
I shall cut my nets,
But what shall I say to my mother,
To whom I go every day
Laden with my catch.
Today I have set no traps
For love of you ensnares me.

If only I were her negress
Who is her constant companion,
Then would I see
The hue of all her limbs.
If only I were her laundryman,
Even for a single month,
Then would I joyfully wash out the unguent
That is on her dress.
If only I were the ring
That is on her finger,
Then I would protect her
Like that which makes her life happy.

And a successful lover is able to exult:

If I kiss her and her lips are open,
Then am I drunk even without beer.

My sister has come, my heart is overjoyed
As I open my arms to embrace her.

My heart pulsates within me
Like the red fish in its pond.
O night go on forever,
Now that my queen has come.[3]

Occasionally, two people in love could persuade even the King of Egypt to change his plans. The story is told on a papyrus now in Cairo Museum of the son and daughter of a pharaoh named Mernebptah.[4] They were his only children and the king proposed to marry his son, Neneferkaptah, to the daughter of a general, and his daughter, Ahwere, to the son of a general. Neneferkaptah and Ahwere loved each other and wanted to marry; and so Ahwere asked her father's chief steward to intercede for her. The steward did so and King Mernebptah became silent and distressed. When the steward asked him why, the king replied,

> It is you who distress me. If it so happens that I have only two children, is it right to marry one to the other? Should I not rather marry Neneferkaptah to the daughter of a general and Ahwere to the son of another general, so that our family may increase!

Her unhappiness caused Ahwere to fall into a decline and lose her looks; but she did not lose her wits, so that when she was summoned to dine with her father she quoted his own words back at him and won her cause. The king set aside his plans, allowing Ahwere and Neneferkaptah to marry each other. An interesting point in this story is that King Mernebptah was upset *not* because he was marrying brother and sister to each other, which in most societies today would be regarded, with repugnance, as incest, but because he was being asked to lose the opportunity of enlarging his family by introducing new members into it in the shape of unrelated children-in-law. It is a common belief that all Egyptians could, if they wished, marry their full sisters or brothers; and some kings are known to have done so. Several kings even married their own daughters (see pages 151, 154, 155). The issue is confused by the fact that in literature men and women, especially those in love, often address each other as 'brother' and 'sister'. It is clear, however, that these terms are usually not to be taken literally; they are simply a way of indicating affection, but not necessarily between siblings.[5]

The Greeks misunderstood the situation, and stated that marriage between brother and sister was normal in ancient Egypt, but this was probably not the case. Among ordinary Egyptians marriage between full sister and brother was rare; although marriage between half brother and sister, that is, the children of the same father but different mothers, was often found in circles where a man could afford several wives or concubines. As far as the royal family was concerned, the answer, given by the royal judges to the Persian king, Cambyses, when he asked them if there was a law which permitted a man to marry his sister, is instructive. They told him that there was no law which permitted that; but 'there was undoubtedly a law which permitted the King of Persia to do what he pleased'.[6] Doubtless, a similar law could have been found for the King of Egypt.

How great a part love played in choosing a marriage partner is not clear: it seems that most marriages in ancient Egypt were arranged. In societies where this is the custom, the choice of spouse is usually made by parents in order to give the greatest social and financial advantages to their offspring. As far as a daughter is concerned, a rich and successful man, even if much older than the prospective bride, is a desirable son-in-law; as is a man able to offer his wife a better position in society than that of her parents. Occasionally a son will be married to an older woman for the same reasons. In modern Egypt a first cousin is considered to be an ideal choice of marriage partner, for reasons of family property. Much the same considerations seem to have prevailed in ancient Egypt, where it appears that marriages between members of the same social class were considered most desirable; and where it was not unusual for marriages to take place between cousins, and even between uncle and niece.[7]

In Egypt today many young people find their own marriage partners, but very often the females in a family look for a suitable young man or woman to be introduced to one of their relatives with a view to marriage; love in these cases being expected to grow with acquaintance. In ancient Egypt, also, the women in a family played an important part in arranging a marriage: it seems that a suitor sometimes used a female go-between or approached the girl's mother (note, not her father) to ask for her support, as the lament of the fictitious heroine of one love poem indicates: 'He does not know of my desire to embrace him, or he would plead with my mother.'[8]

In ancient Egypt, marriage was regarded as highly desirable by both men and women. As in most countries, both ancient and modern, marriage, motherhood and home-making were the principal occupations to which the majority of women aspired, but men also appreciated the benefits of being married. The sage, Ptahhotep, who probably lived in the latter half of the Sixth Dynasty (*c.* 2345–2181 BC), encouraged young men to get married and proffered them the following advice on how to treat their wives:

> When you prosper, set up a household for yourself. Love your wife passionately, as is proper. Fill her belly, clothe her back. Soothe her body with perfumed oil. Gladden her heart as long as you live, for she is a fertile field for her lord.

To which he added a salutary warning:

> Never contend with her in court . . . and keep her from gaining the upper hand![9]

Many Egyptians seem to have embarked on marriage at what, to us, seems to be an early age – usually fifteen for boys, twelve for girls,[10] although Ankhsheshonq's (see page 12) advice was to 'take a wife when you are twenty years old, that you may have a son when you are young.' However, ancient Egyptians, like their modern descendants, matured early and until quite recently marriage at these ages among the *fellahin* (peasants) was not unusual; nor was it unusual, for instance, in medieval Britain. The average life span for women in ancient Egypt and in medieval Britain was about the same – eighteen to twenty years; thus early maturity was a biological necessity. In any case, in a society where the only real choice for most girls was between remaining in their parents' home or leaving it only on marriage, it is not surprising that early marriage, with its promise of at least a measure of independence, was something to be looked forward to.

An ancient Egyptian woman's attitude towards, and expectations of, marriage might well have been envied by women in many ancient societies, as they might also have been by those in Victorian Britain and other modern societies. The following speech written by Sophocles in the fifth century BC epitomizes the despair that many women of his own and other times must have felt on marriage:

> But now outside my father's house I am nothing. Yes, often have I looked on the nature of women thus, that we are nothing. Young girls, in my opinion, have the sweetest existence known to mortals in their father's homes, for innocence keeps children safe and happy always. But when we reach puberty and understanding, we are thrust out and sold away from our ancestral gods and from our parents. Some go to strangers' homes, others to foreigners', some to joyless houses, some to hostile. And all this, once the first night has yoked us to our husband, we are forced to praise and say that all is well.[11]

In contrast, an ancient Egyptian woman, especially one from the propertied classes, need not fear that like Congreve's Millamant she would 'by degrees dwindle into a wife'[12] and become a mere chattel of her husband; her status under the law, which, as we saw in Chapter Two, was considerable, was not lost on marriage.

The rites and customs attendant upon marriage in, say, western Christian society, that is, a ceremony, which may be secular or religious, performed under the auspices of a recognized body; a period of betrothal or engagement; an exchange of engagement and wedding rings; and, in some societies, the drawing up of a marriage contract, were, with the exception of the marriage contract, apparently not a part of the celebration of marriage in ancient Egypt. It seems, to the ancient Egyptians, that marriage was simply 'the intention of making a way in life together',[13] with the assumption that in order to bring this about the wife must live in the same house as her husband.

The phrase most often used to indicate marriage was *rdi n A B m ḥmt*, ('to give to A (man's name) B (woman's name) as wife'). Documents[14] show that from the New Kingdom, if not before, until the Twenty-sixth Dynasty, a girl in normal circumstances was given in marriage by her father: the last known instance of this is dated to 548 BC.[15] But a document dating to 536 BC[16] marks a change in practice: from that time onwards, all documents drawn up to record a marriage use the formula 'The man has said to the woman "I have taken you as a wife" '.[17] The phrase *iri n ḥmt*, 'to take as wife',[18] was of course for use by a man; there seems to have been no equivalent phrase for use by a woman.

The commonest word for 'marry' was *mni*; but this word also meant moor a ship or attach to a cult-service. The words 'moor' and 'attach' can, of course, be used metaphorically in reference to marriage; but it is to be hoped that another meaning of *mni*, 'die', was never used in this way! *ḳ r pr*, 'to enter a house', was often used with the meaning 'to marry'[19]; as was *ḥmsi r-c*, 'to sit with'.[20]

Another term used to indicate marriage was *grg pr*, or 'set up a household', and this perhaps is an indication of what marriage meant in ancient Egypt: the setting up of a communal household. When Ahwere (see page 56) married her Neneferkaptah, there was no marriage ceremony, even between this royal couple. Her father simply ordered that she 'be taken to the house of Neneferkaptah tonight', and further commanded, 'let all kinds of beautiful things be taken with her.' Ahwere herself said,

> I was taken as a wife to the house of Neneferkaptah. Pharaoh commanded that I should have a great dowry of gold and silver, and all the members of the royal household gave me presents. Neneferkaptah made merry with me, and entertained all the royal household. He slept with me that night and found me pleasing. He slept with me again and again and we loved each other.

Ahwere's marriage has certain similarities with marriage in Egypt today. Like many modern brides she was taken to her husband's house in the evening; and just as a bride today has her furniture taken from her parents' home to her new home, so Ahwere had 'all kinds of beautiful things' to take with her. Neneferkaptah 'entertained all the royal household' (who would have been men) – his version of a stag night.

From Ahwere's account, it would seem that it was not deemed necessary for Neneferkaptah and his bride to appear before officials to mark their marriage. In the case of ordinary Egyptians, however, some formal recognition was probably necessary – not in the shape of any kind of ceremony, religious or secular, or for legal reasons, since the state regarded the actual marriage as a private matter, but for the sake of financial concerns to do with property: the marriage settlement (see page 63) was an important part of an ancient Egyptian marriage – yet another meaning of the word *mni* was 'endow'.

In ancient Egypt an important part of getting married was probably an appearance before officials, who noted the names of the couple and recorded the details of the marriage settlement. Up to the Twenty-sixth Dynasty it seems usually to have been the groom and the father of the bride who made the appearance; after that time, the bride in person is party to the settlement.[21] The marriage settlement was solely concerned with questions of property: as far as we know, at no time did it refer to the behaviour and duties of the spouses towards each other. There is one known example, however, of a father in the Twentieth Dynasty who tried to ensure his daughter's welfare: 'Make Nekhwemmut take the oath, saying that he will not treat my daughter badly.'[22]

Muslim marriage in modern Egypt bears a marked resemblance to that of the ancient Egyptians. For Egyptian Muslims, there is no religious ceremony on marriage, which is not regarded as a sacrament. For them, the definition of marriage is a contract between a man and a woman based on free acceptance by both parties, although each will have been given much advice by their respective families. There is a marriage deed, which is considered to be a contract of agreement since it binds two equal parties; and each party has the right to state his or her conditions in the contract, which is binding on them both. The marriage deed must be notarized; and both parties must appear before the notary public to record the notarization. In certain circumstances, a delegate may be given power of attorney to act for one of the parties – very often the woman – although good cause must be given for this. The actual marriage is enacted by the bride going to her husband's house.

On marriage, an ancient Egyptian man became a *hy* (alternative writing: *h3y*) 'husband' and gained for himself a household and a wife who, he hoped, would bear him children and run the household competently. A woman became a *hmt*, 'wife' and was given the title *nbt hwt* or 'mistress of the house',[23] for the house was considered to be her special domain. She did not change her name on marriage (in ancient Egypt there was no family name), nor did she lose control of her property. Normally, she would expect to be her husband's only wife, although polygamy was not unknown (see page 67). Sometimes, the term used for 'wife' was not *hmt* but *hbsyt*; but what, if any, was the legal distinction between the two terms is not known. The same problem arises with the terms *iw.s m hmt n* and *iw.s m-dî*, translated respectively as 'who is wife of' and 'who is with'. Attempts have been made to classify marriages of different legal status and type, but these have not been successful.[24]

In due course a wife would share her husband's tomb; and in reliefs and statue groups in that tomb she would be depicted as more or less the same size as her husband, an artistic convention that meant that she was considered to be of equal importance. In the inscriptions on the walls of the tomb or on statue bases her name is often prefixed with *mrt.f*, 'his beloved', indicating that affection was the norm between husband and wife. The lady of the house was treated with respect by servants, family and, not least, by her husband. It is perhaps salutary to note that nowhere in the *Wisdom Literature*, or elsewhere, is a man advised to beat his wife or to teach her to be obedient to him. Statues of family groups, with wives sitting side by side with their husbands, arms placed affectionately round their waists, and their children, both sons and daughters, at their feet, proclaim the devotion of the Egyptians to a happy family life.

When members of the propertied classes married, a document variously called *' n hmt* or *dm' n hmt* or, most often, *sh n hmt*, was drawn up. The literal translation of each of the above phrases is 'a document concerning a wife', which scholars often interpret as 'marriage contract'. It is probably safer, however, not to use the term marriage contract since this expression has different meanings under different legal systems: under French law, for example, a *contrat de mariage* is concerned with property rights, while under Italian canonical law, a *contratto di matrimonio* is required in order to validate a marriage. It seems safer, therefore, to translate *sh n hmt*, and the other Egyptian phrases mentioned above, as 'marriage settlement'.

A marriage settlement was essentially to do with property rights and the arrangements made with regard to property in connection with a marriage: it in no way served as proof of marriage, nor was it a legal requirement.[25] Such formal settlements were not made by members of the poorest classes, who would have found the cost of hiring a scribe to draw up the document prohibitive[26] and in any case had little property to dispose of. Although, not unexpectedly, most of the examples of marriage settlements extant, and indeed of any documentary evidence regarding the legal aspects of marriage, date to the later years of ancient Egyptian history, there is no reason to suppose that they are untypical of the arrangements of earlier years. Marriage settlements were usually drawn up between a woman's father and her prospective husband, although sometimes the woman herself was the contracting partner. The higher the social status of the woman the greater were the demands in the way of financial and legal safeguards for her.

The settlements have a standard form:[27]

The date (i.e. the year of reign of the ruling monarch).
The two contractors (the future husband and wife) are named.
The parents of both are named.
The husband's profession, occupation or origin is always noted; the wife's hardly ever.
The scribe who drew up the contract is named.
The names of the witnesses are given. (There can be between three and thirty-six witnesses; in the Ptolemaic Period the number is regularly sixteen.)[28]

Then follow the details of the settlement.

A copy of the marriage settlement was given into the safekeeping of
a disinterested party or placed in the archives of a temple.

An example of a marriage settlement dating to 219 BC is quoted
below:

> The Blemmyan, born in Egypt, Horemheb, son of Horpais, whose
> mother is Wenis, has said to the woman Tais, daughter of
> Khahor, whose mother is Tairetdjeret: I have made you a married
> woman. As your woman's portion [*šp n šḥmt*; see below], I give you
> two pieces of silver . . . If I dismiss you as wife and dislike you and
> prefer another woman to you as wife, I will give you two pieces of
> silver in addition to the two pieces of silver mentioned above,
> which I have given to you as your woman's portion . . .
> And I will give you one third of each and everything that will
> accrue to you and me.
> The children which you bear me are heirs to [lit: lords of] each
> and everything that I possess, and that I have yet to acquire. Your
> eldest son is my eldest son of the children you have borne to me
> and which you will bear to me.
> Here is the list of your dowry [*nkwt n šḥmt*, lit: 'goods of a
> woman']²⁹ which you have brought with you into my house:
> 1 *inšn*-cloth³⁰ to the value of 6 *kite* [approx. 54 grammes] of silver;
> 6 *kite* of copper; 1 bracelet to the value of 2 *kite* [approx.
> 18 grammes] of silver; 1 wig in the name of your portion
> [mentioned] above, which I have not given to you, to the value of
> 2 pieces of silver.
> Total value of your dowry which you have brought with you into
> my house: in copper money – [the worth of] 3 silver coins and
> 4 *kite* [36 grammes approx.]
> I shall not be able to say about your dowry described above, 'No,
> you did not bring it into my house with you. . . . I have received it
> from your hand complete and intact; I am satisfied with it.
> If I dismiss you, or if you should wish to leave, then I will give
> back to you the dowry that you have brought with you into my
> house, or the monetary value of it according to the price detailed
> above. The right to dispose of it belongs to me.
> Written by [the scribe] Tayenimu, son of Pabenerfy.

On the verso of the document are the names of sixteen witnesses.[31]

An interesting point about the marriage settlement above, and others, is the *šp n shmt*, a gift made by the husband to the wife, which consisted usually of a small amount of money and sometimes a quantity of corn.[32] Its origins are unknown but it is reasonable to suppose that the *šp* began as compensation to a father for the loss of his daughter's services – a sort of brideprice; and the translation of *šp n shmt* is perhaps best rendered as 'the compensation for making [a woman] a wife'. The oldest examples extant of the *šp* date only to the Twenty-fifth and Twenty-sixth Dynasties, but it seems clear that by that time the *šp* was no longer paid to the father but to the woman herself. From about 230 BC, the *šp* became a fictitious payment that only had to be made in reality if the marriage were dissolved.

One type of marriage settlement that was very favourable to the wife was the *sh n s'nh*, the literal translation of which is 'document of causing to live', in other words, a maintenance document. Most of the examples known so far come from Memphis, Thebes and Siut, the earliest of them dating to 361 BC, although the earliest known documents using the phrase *sh n s'nh* date to between 563 BC and 522 BC, to the reigns of Amasis and Cambyses.[33] In a maintenance document, a husband undertook to support his wife in every way, and to pay her an allowance, calculated annually but paid monthly: the following example, dating to 181 BC, is typical:

> I give you 125 *artabas* [about 3,750 kilos] of bedet [emmer wheat] and 5 pieces of silver from the treasury of Ptah, my payment for your clothes [the normal phrase is 'for your food and clothes']. . . . You are entitled to arrears [in payment] of your maintenance, which will be at my charge: I shall give it to you. . . . Everything that I possess and that I shall acquire is a security for your *s'nh*.[34]

An element of maintenance had long been a feature of marriage in ancient Egypt, as can be seen in Ptahhotep's injunction to a man to fill the belly and clothe the back of his wife (see page 58). Diodorus, for one, did not approve of what he took to be the stranglehold that Egyptian women had over their husbands, and sourly noted that 'The wife lords it over the husband as in the deed about the maintenance, the men agree to obey the wife in every-thing.'[35] However, the arrangements were often between equal partners and could work both ways: several papyri, of which the earliest dates to 517 BC, record that women have handed over large sums of money to their husbands as payment for the rights and privileges that they will be granted during the marriage.[36]

One of the main reasons for marriage was the begetting of children. Just as a Muslim Egyptian man today wishes for a son who will say the prayers for him at his death, so an ancient Egyptian desired a son who would in the fullness of time be responsible for his burial. And so the sage, Ani, in the Eighteenth Dynasty, proffered the following advice:

Take a wife when you are young, so that she might give you a son. She should bear him for you while you are still young, then you will [live to] see him become a man. Happy is the man with a large family, for he is respected on account of his children.[37]

The arrival of a son, or even a daughter, to a married couple could not, unfortunately, be guaranteed, and some men preferred to arrange a 'year of eating', a trial marriage,[38] in order to ascertain whether a woman could have children. In these cases, a contract would be drawn up similar to the following:

Psenmin, son of Khensthoth, says to Tamin, daughter of Pamont: four *deben* [364 grammes] of refined silver have I given to you before the goddesses Hathor and Rattowe. You shall be in my house, being with me as wife, from today, Year 16, third month of the second season, first day, until Year 17, fourth month of the first season, first day [i.e. nine months].
If you go away to your own house [before the end of the nine months] you shall pay back the four *deben* of refined silver.
If it should so happen that I be the one who makes you leave, I shall forfeit the four *deben* of refined silver that I have already paid into the hands of the agents of Psenamy, the money changer and agent.[39]

According to Diodorus,[40] all Egyptians, apart from priests, practised polygamy: Herodotus, in contrast, stated that like the Greeks the Egyptians were monogamous.[41] It seems likely that Herodotus was the more correct and that, with the exception of kings who, for dynastic reasons, often had many wives, polygamy was rare in ancient Egypt. The case is difficult to prove because such evidence as there is, is often ambiguous: take, for example, a papyrus of the Twentieth Dynasty which refers to 'The citizeness A, the wife of B, and the citizeness C, his other wife, in total 2'.[42] The reference may be to two contemporaneous wives; on the other hand, wife A may have been divorced or dead before B married wife C – there is nothing to indicate which was the real state of affairs.

Reference is often made to more than one wife in funerary stelae; and reliefs and statue groups often show a man with two or more wives. In the majority of cases, there is no indication that the man was married to all of these wives simultaneously. In inscriptions, the phrase *ḥmt.f ḥr-ḥ3t*, 'his former wife' may be used, but absence of this phrase does not necessarily indicate that a man was married to several women at once. The most that can be said in such cases is that the women appearing in the reliefs or statue groups are hardly likely to be divorced wives; and that where several women appear with one man, each one (except the last) is more likely to be a wife who predeceased her husband, who then married again.

Cases of what can only be construed as polygamy are known among the bureaucratic classes in the Middle Kingdom;[43] and there are several attested examples from the New Kingdom, notably in papyri concerning the great tomb robberies of the Twentieth Dynasty. One of these,[44] for example, concerns the case of a goldworker named Ramose, who lived about 1100 BC. When his wife, Mutemhab, was questioned at the robbery tribunal, she mentioned that her husband had had two wives who were both dead, but that a third was still alive. Ramose was eventually brought to trial, but for tomb robbery, not polygamy! It seems clear that although polygamy was rare in ancient Egypt, it was not officially proscribed. On the other hand it is safe to assume that women were not so equal in ancient Egypt that they were ever encouraged to practise polyandry!

In ancient Egypt it was permissible for a man, even if married, to have as many concubines as he could afford and could persuade the other ladies of his household, especially his wife, to accept. It seems reasonable to suppose that he would first seek his wife's consent to the arrangement, since she might feel that the arrival in her household of a rival for her husband's affections constituted grounds for divorce (see page 70). Judging from prayers found inscribed in certain tombs which ask for the reunification after death of a man, his wife, his children, his parents *and* his concubines, the arrangement seems often to have proved a happy one.

Legally, if not always domestically, the status of a married man's concubine did not match that of his wife. For this reason it seems probable that any woman in a position to bring property to a partnership, and therefore able to demand marriage, was not likely to forego the privileges of a wife for the lesser status of concubine.

Permitted concubines apart, a wife could expect her husband to be faithful to her, for infidelity in a married man was not considered socially acceptable; neither was philandering, even among bachelors, if the protestations of denial to the contrary are anything to go by. A certain Amenemhet swears on his funerary stela 'I did not know the slave girl in [my father's] house. I did not seduce his maid servant.'[45] Another man, in a letter written to his dead wife, declares: 'You never saw me deceiving you like a peasant, going to another house . . . Look, I have spent three years on my own without going to another house, although it is by no means comfortable to have to do so. But look, I did it for your sake. And look, as for the women in the house, I did not have intercourse with them.'[46]

In Herodotus's time, Egyptian women were renowned for infidelity. In his *Histories*, he recounted the presumably apocryphal story of a king who went blind but, having been blind for ten years, was told by an oracle that he would recover his sight if he bathed his eyes in the urine of a woman who had never lain with any man except her husband:

> He tried his wife first, but without success – he remained as blind as ever; then he tried other women, a great many, one after another, until at last his sight was restored. Then he collected

within the walls of a town, now called Red Clod, all the women except the one whose urine had proved efficacious, set the place on fire, and burnt them to death, town and all; afterwards he married the woman who had been the means of curing him.[47]

It might be expected in a society where property passed through the female line that adultery on the part of a wife would be considered a heinous crime. Diodorus, at least, seems to confirm this; and also that it was a serious matter for a man, for he noted that if a man committed adultery with the woman's consent, the law required that he should receive a thousand blows with the rod, and that the woman should have her nose cut off.[48] How far this was Diodorus's opinion of what *should* be a punishment for adultery rather than what was actually the practice is difficult to ascertain. Certainly, the norm in ancient Egyptian literature was that adultery resulted in death – even attempted adultery as in the Story of the Two Brothers (see page 15).

One literary example of what an adulterous wife might expect is found in the Westcar Papyrus, in the story told by Prince Khafre of the wife of Webaoner, a chief lector-priest.[49] She fell in love with a commoner and sent him a box filled with clothing. One day, the commoner asked Webaoner's wife to come down to the summerhouse in the garden with him, and she ordered the head gardener to make it ready for them. They spent the day there together, drinking and making love. At the end of the day, the wife's lover went down to the pool to bathe. Unfortunately for the lovers, the head gardener told the deceived husband about the affair. Thereupon, Webaoner made a wax crocodile and ordered the gardener to throw it into the pool the next time his wife's lover went down to bathe. And so it was done. The wax crocodile turned into a real crocodile, seven cubits long, which seized the lover and carried him down to the bottom of the pool.

As for the wife. When the matter was reported to the king, he ordered

the wife of Webaoner to be taken to a plot of land on the north side of the Royal Residence, where fire was heaped upon her. Her ashes were then thrown into the river.

The fate of the two lovers was indeed terrible, given that, according to ancient Egyptian belief, the preservation of the body in as lifelike a shape as possible and housed correctly within a tomb was necessary for a life after death. The commoner might have expected his punishment, especially since he had dallied with the wife of an important man; but the fact that Webaoner's wife, a member of the upper classes, was punished in such a harsh way and made to forfeit her hopes of the Afterlife, shows how serious a matter adultery was for a woman. At least it was in this story, in which the fate of the adulterers was perhaps being used solely as a cautionary tale about people who deviated from the expectations of ideal behaviour, rather than as a reflection of what happened in real life.

Adultery was not approved of; but in the normal course of events it seems that the state regarded adultery as a domestic matter and took no interest in meting out punishment for it, except perhaps financially. In some marriage settlements, the earliest-known of which date from sometime after 1000 BC, there are clauses which punish the 'heavy sin' of adultery in a *woman* by simply depriving her of her financial rights.[50] An adulterous *man*, on the other hand, who was having an affair with a married woman, might expect his punishment to come from the aggrieved husband. Ankhsheshonq advised, 'Do not make love to a married woman. He who makes love to a married woman is killed on her doorstep'[51] – not, presumably, by agents of the state. His advice to a cuckolded husband is simple: 'If you find your wife with her lover, get yourself a bride to suit you.'[52]

When a marriage broke down divorce was possible, and could be initiated either by the wife or by the husband. Like marriage and adultery, divorce was a private matter in which the state took no interest; and it seems that at no time was it considered to be socially unacceptable. The actual divorce was simple: a man had merely to recite the following formula before witnesses:

I have dismissed you as wife, I have abandoned you, I have no claim on earth upon you. I have said to you, 'Take a husband for yourself in any place to which you will go'.[53]

However easy a divorce was in theory, in practice it was often less so. Social, financial and family pressures may sometimes have militated against a couple divorcing; and the settlement that had been drawn up before the marriage may have stipulated financial penalties that were so harsh that legal separation was impractical.

The most common reasons for a husband to 'dismiss' his wife were her inability to bear children or, more especially, to provide him with a son; his wish to marry someone else; or the fact that she simply ceased to please him. What a woman thought about being set aside, simply because she had ceased to please the man with whom she lived, is summed up in a famous but perhaps apocryphal case from the records of Deir el-Medina (see page 7): not, in this instance, concerning a wife, but rather a concubine, who nevertheless was as scornful of the move as any wife would have been:

> The case of the woman who was blind in one eye, and who was in the house of one man for twenty years: he found another woman, and he said to her, ''I shall throw you out for you are blind in one eye.' So it is said. And she said to him, 'Has it taken my being in your house for twenty years for you to find that out?'[54]

A wife might divorce her husband for cruelty, either physical or, in modern parlance, mental. Although it seems to have been accepted that a husband might beat his wife, he was not allowed to do it to excess. If she considered that he had abused the right, a wife could take her husband before a tribunal and complain. After that, he was usually given a warning: but if he ignored it, then he could be sentenced to a hundred lashes; and, in addition, would have to forfeit everything that his wife had contributed to their joint estate, as, for example, in this case from the Twentieth Dynasty:

> If I shall ever treat the daughter of Tenermentu unjustly again, I shall receive 100 strokes and be deprived of everything that I shall have acquired with her.[55]

If a man divorced his wife, he had to return her dowry (*nkwt n shmt*; see page 64) and give her the 'marriage portion' (*šp n shmt*; see page 65) that had been agreed in their marriage settlement; and he had also to pay her compensation and give her a share (usually a third, but sometimes a half) of any property that they had acquired during their marriage, as the following document from 264 BC illustrates:

> If I repudiate you as wife, if I take a dislike to you and want another wife, I shall give you 5 *deben* [455 grammes] of silver . . . and I shall give you half of all and everything that I possess and that I shall acquire together with you from this day and after-wards.[56]

If, however, the divorce originated with the wife, then she seems to have forfeited her right to a share of the communal property[57] and she was the one who paid compensation – one lady from about 340 BC made the following undertaking:

> If I repudiate you as my husband, if I take a dislike to you and want someone else, I shall give you two and a half *kite* [about 22 grammes] of silver; and forfeit the third part of all and everything that I shall acquire together with you.[58]

Once divorced, both men and women could remarry as soon as they wished; and the fact that many of them did so, if not perhaps an example of the triumph of hope over experience, is testimony to the value that ancient Egyptians placed upon marriage.

CHAPTER FIVE

HEALTH AND CHILDBIRTH

Ancient Egyptians of both sexes suffered from the same health problems as the *fellahin* of today: rheumatism and arthritis; other aches and pains caused by damp living and working conditions; intestinal infections due to impure water; intestinal worms; and bilharzia, caused by blood flukes of the *Schistosomidae* family which enter the body through the soles of the feet via the water in the ditches and canals in which the victims work. They also suffered from dermatitis, boils, sores and animal bites, which could become infected; and from mastoid and naso-pharyngeal diseases, as well as ophthalmia and other eye complaints caused by friction from sand and dust, irritation from the sun and infection carried by flies and other insects. Sand and dust also caused lung diseases, particularly sand pneumoconiosis. Other respiratory disorders such as emphysema were common, as were disorders of the alimentary tract, especially renal calculi and gall-stones.

Medicine was one of the oldest professions in Egypt, and Egyptian doctors enjoyed a high reputation in the ancient world. The earliest 'doctor' was a magician, for the Egyptians believed that disease and sickness were caused by an evil force entering the body: it was thought, for example, that the west wind carried disease; and that the breath of life entered by the right ear but that the breath of death came into the left ear. The Egyptians subscribed to the theory of 'possession' by evil forces, and believed that they could be 'fought with', 'driven out' or 'killed' by means of threats, curses and spells. To this end, they employed sympathetic magic – laying a figurine on the patient to 'absorb' the sickness, for example. The same theory lay behind the medicines that these magicians prescribed, which were made up of concoctions so revolting that the evil spirits, unable to endure them, would be driven out. However, it was inevitable that some of these concoctions inadvertently contained efficacious ingredients; and, at an early stage in Egyptian history, many magicians began to concentrate on prescriptions of proved efficiency in certain circumstances. Thus, some magicians became real doctors, their magic, real medicine. At no time, however, did medicine oust magic entirely. One was employed alongside the other, with medicine being used to treat ailments that had obvious human or natural causes (broken bones, for instance) and magic for all ailments whose cause was not evident (aches, pains, sores). Sympathetic magic continued in use – for example, migraine was treated by laying a fried fish on the side of the head.[1]

The ancient Egyptian word for doctor was *sinw*; and we know of four categories of specialist: the *sinw irt* or eye doctor; the *sinw ht* or belly doctor; the *sinw ibh* or tooth doctor; and the picturesquely-named *nrw phwt* or 'shepherd of the hindquarters', a most necessary branch of medicine in a society in which intestinal troubles were endemic. There was no specific term for gynaecologist: all doctors were apparently prepared to deal with gynaecological problems.

Doctors were also known as *w'bw Shmt* – the 'pure ones [i.e. priests] of the [goddess] Sekhmet'. Sekhmet was a lion-headed goddess who was thought to aid her priests to drive out the demons which caused sickness. Doctors were trained in her temples; and, in fact, the ancient Egyptian medical service was centred on temples throughout the land, not solely those of Sekhmet but also of other deities. In theory, treatment was free; but it can be imagined that ability to make gifts to the doctor might have some bearing on the availability and quality of treatment. In the lower classes especially, men's labour was considered more valuable than women's; it was men, therefore, who were the more likely to receive medical treatment, except when it came to a question of the safe delivery of a baby, in which case a woman might expect that her husband and family would try to arrange for her to consult a doctor if necessary. In the thirteenth century BC, at least one man thought it worthy of note that he had arranged for a doctor to see his wife. In a letter written after her death, he reminded her:

> And when you fell ill of that sickness which you suffered, I caused
> to be sent to you a master physician, and he treated you and did
> all of which you said, 'Do it!'[2]

According to Clement of Alexandria (AD 200), the Egyptians had
forty-two books containing the sum total of human knowledge.
Among these books were six on medicine, of which one dealt with
'diseases of women'. No original examples of these works have
survived, but a considerable number of medical papyri[3] are nevertheless extant, some of which deal in varying degrees with 'diseases
of women'. The oldest-known medical papyrus was discovered in
1898 at El-Lahun (today called Kahun) by Flinders Petrie: it is now
known as the Kahun Papyrus,[4] named after the site at which it was
found. The Kahun Papyrus dates from about 1880 BC, but it is
certainly a copy of a much older text. Its first two pages contain
seventeen gynaecological prescriptions and instructions; and it is
worthy of note that surgical methods are not included in the
instructions. On the third page are seventeen prescriptions for the
assessment of sterility and pregnancy, and for ascertaining the sex
of an unborn child. Much of the Kahun Papyrus deals unashamedly
in magic spells, although it does contain some accurate observations; and it can be considered as the first textbook of gynaecology
in medical history.

The most important of all the medical papyri is the one which
was purchased in Luxor in 1873 by the German Egyptologist, Georg
Ebers, and thenceforward called the Ebers Papyrus.[5] Dating from
the reign of Amenhotep I (1526–1505 BC) the Ebers Papyrus is over
65 feet long and contains 108 pages. Its opening lines read 'Here
begins the book on the preparation of medicine for all parts of the
human body', and apart from sections dealing with diseases of the
stomach, and surgical treatment for boils, carbuncles and cysts, the
Ebers Papyrus has a section on gynaecology, the most interesting
part of which gives remedies for a prolapsed uterus, a condition
that has been observed in several Egyptian mummies. It also deals
with gonorrhea, contraception, assistance in childbirth, and with

what is thought to be cancer – called in the papyrus 'eating in the womb'. The Ebers Papyrus is distinguished from other medical papyri in the way in which it deals with medicine in an objective and material way, without resorting to magic.

Another important medical papyrus dates from about 1600 BC and is named after the American Egyptologist who purchased it in 1862. The Edwin Smith Papyrus,[6] which is over 15 feet long, was translated over a period of ten years by the doyen of American Egyptology, James Henry Breasted, who published it in 1930. He proved that it was a copy of a much older text – one probably dating to between 2500 and 2000 BC – for many of the words used in it were no longer in current usage at the time it was prepared but date in fact from the Old Kingdom (c. 2680–2180 BC). The Edwin Smith Papyrus is chiefly a textbook of surgery; its main section is entitled 'The Book of Wounds', but there is a smaller section on gynaecology.

There are several other medical papyri which contain sections on gynaecology, although they are less important than those outlined above. They are the Carlsberg VIII[7] and the Chester Beatty (named after their first modern owners); the Ramesseum Papyri (named after the site at which they were discovered); and the Berlin Papyrus (named after the city where it is kept today). The Chester Beatty Medical Papyri, which date from the Nineteenth Dynasty (1315–1200 BC), are now in the British Museum: the most important of them, Number VI, has a section on gynaecological problems, while Number X concerns aphrodisiacs. There are three Ramesseum Papyri, also in the British Museum, dating to the Twelfth Dynasty (1991–1786 BC): one of them contains spells and prescriptions for pregnant women and newly-born children. The Berlin Papyrus (Nineteenth Dynasty) is mainly concerned with childbirth and contraception, and the protection of the newborn baby; and it also has a section on fertility tests.

Most of the lesser medical papyri, and the gynaecological sections of the more important ones, cover much the same ground as the Kahun Papyrus; the formulae employed in them are so similar, both to each other and to those in the Kahun Papyrus, that it seems likely that they all derive from the same source. The Kahun

Papyrus is the oldest and most complete version of that source. Typically, it records observations of individual cases, which are set out in a standard way: the title of the case is given (for example, 'Treatment of a woman suffering from . . .'); then follows the examination (symptoms described); then the diagnosis is given ('Say with regard to it . . .'); finally, treatment is prescribed:

> [title]: Instructions for a woman suffering in her neck, pubic parts and ears.
> [examination]: She does not hear what is said to her.
> [diagnosis]: You should say about her: 'This is a disturbance of the womb'.
> [treatment]: You should prescribe for it the same prescription as that for driving out discharges of the womb.[8]

No surgical treatment is prescribed in the Kahun Papyrus; or, for that matter, in any of the other gynaecological papyri.

The ancient Egyptians were justly famed for the quality of their medical knowledge – in Homer's opinion 'in medical knowledge the Egyptian leaves the rest of the world behind'[9] – but they had their limitations. It is very doubtful if true operative surgery was practised at all, for it is clear that to the Egyptians the vessels leading to and from the heart were not exclusively concerned with the carriage of blood but were the vehicles for air, water, semen, mucus and other secretions. This would seem to indicate that their observations were made on dead bodies – presumably during mummification – and not by opening up the living. The Egyptians possessed over a hundred anatomical terms which between them gave a fairly accurate description of the body in general, but they described the nerves, muscles, veins and arteries by a single word – *mtw*; and the terms used are the same as those employed to describe the anatomy of animals.

The medical papyri indicate that ancient Egyptian physicians treated patients suffering from rheumatoid and arthritic complaints; diseases of the lungs, liver, stomach, intestines and bladder; afflictions of the ear, nose, throat, mouth, tongue and teeth; and afflictions of the head and scalp (including alopecia). They also dealt in ointments for the prevention of falling or greying hair, beauty treatments and aphrodisiacs; and offered household remedies for getting rid of flies, fleas, snakes and other vermin. An addendum, at the end of the great Edwin Smith Papyrus, contains a formula for the rejuvenation of old people, which, as a matter of interest, is an extraction of fenugreek for the elimination of wrinkles!

In general the Egyptians, especially when young, had good, strong, white teeth. Examinations of mummies, however, have revealed that by adulthood, many ancient Egyptians of both sexes were suffering from alveolar bone diseases, dental attrition, abcesses and caries. Gum diseases were particularly prevalent among the poorer classes, while among richer Egyptians, caries was the chief scourge. One of the main causes of dental caries today is sugar, which the ancient Egyptians did not possess; affluent ancient Egyptians owed their caries to the fact that the food they ate was much richer and softer than that eaten by the poorer classes. It was the bread eaten by all Egyptians which was the main cause of gum diseases.

Bread in ancient Egypt was very coarse: the grain, from which it was made, was threshed on an earth or stone threshing-floor, so that particles of stone inevitably found their way into it; it was then ground on a stone quern, and to hasten the process of producing flour, small amounts of sand were mixed into the grain. The dough was prepared in an open courtyard, and the poorer Egyptians especially ate the bread out of doors; and anyone who has eaten sandwiches on the seashore will know how thoroughly sand permeates them. The ancient Egyptians ate a great deal of bread, so much of it that the Greeks called them *artophagoi* (bread swallowers). By chewing large amounts of coarse bread contaminated with particles of sand and stone, the ancient Egyptians damaged their gums, thus exposing them to infection; and gradually wore down their teeth, so that wear of the teeth became a common abnormality in their dentition.

Although the ancient Egyptians had a *sinw ibḥ*, or tooth doctor (see page 74), it is doubtful whether he was a true dentist. An artificial tooth with a wooden pivot, mounted on an existing stump, is reputed to have been found during one excavation; and Belzoni, the nineteenth-century explorer, is said to have found false teeth made

Plate 1   Pottery cosmetic vase from the New Kingdom, shaped in
the form of a woman playing a lute
Courtesy of the Trustees of the British Museum

Plate 2   Ramesses III and his daughters, Medinet Habu temple

Plate 3   Granite statue of
Hatshepsut, temple of Amun,
Karnak

Plate 4   Hunting in marshes, tomb of Nakht, Thebes, Eighteenth
Dynasty

Plate 5 *Above:* Spinning and
weaving, from the tomb of
Khnumhotep, Beni Hasan,
Twelfth Dynasty

Plate 6 *Left:* Wooden servant
statue, 20 in high, Eleventh
Dynasty

Plate 7   Guests at feast, tomb of Nebamun, Thebes, Eighteenth Dynasty (now in British Museum)

Plate 8   Musicians and dancers, tomb of Nebamun

Plate 9   Dresses from Deshasheh,
Fifth Dynasty
Courtesy of University College London

Plate 10   Grinding flour: servant statue from Giza, Fifth Dynasty

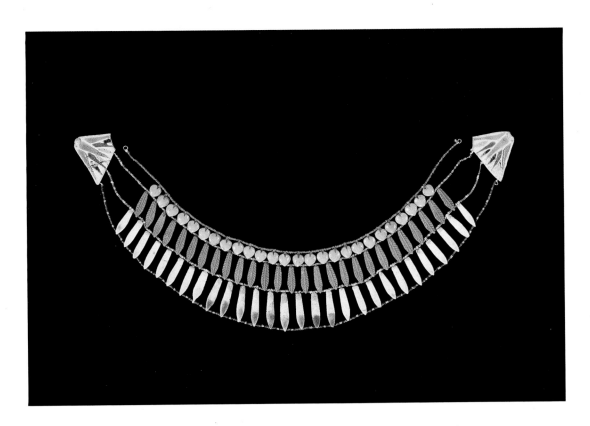

Plate 11   Beaded necklace from el-Amarna, 20 in long, Eighteenth
Dynasty
Courtesy of the Trustees of the British Museum

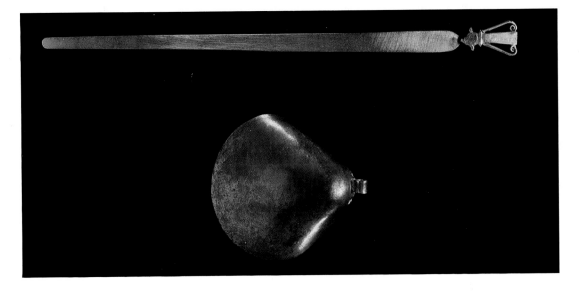

Plate 12   Gold, Bat-headed, hair pin dating to the Twelfth or
Thirteenth Dynasty
Courtesy of Fitzwilliam Museum

Plate 13   Elysian fields from the tomb of Sennedjem, Deir el-Medina, Nineteenth Dynasty

of ivory and wood, fixed by gold bars. Neither of these examples of Egyptian dentistry has survived. At Giza, the German Egyptologist, Hermann Junker, found two teeth linked by a thin gold chain, which he presumed was in order to preserve a loose tooth. However, modern examination[10] of the wire has not revealed the presence of deposits such as tartar, which would seem to indicate that the wire was put into the mouth after the owner of the teeth had died. If this were so, then the operation would have been done to hold the tooth in place for the Afterlife.

The medical papyri contain a series of remedies for the consolidation of the teeth and for the treatment of inflammation and bleeding of the gums. The Ebers Papyrus, for example, advocates that holes in the teeth should be stopped or 'filled' with resin, or chyrysocoll ('Nubian earth').[11] How much was understood of the causes of dental disease and decay may perhaps be judged by the fact that in the Anastasi Papyrus, the cause of caries is ascribed to a worm, a theory also subscribed to by the Assyrians:

> After Anu made the heavens, the heavens made the earth, the earth made the rivers, the rivers made the canals, the canals made the marsh, the marsh made the Worm. The Worm came weeping unto Samas, came unto Ea, her tears flowing: 'What will you give me for my food, what will you give me to destroy?' 'I will give you dried figs and apricots.' 'What use are these dried figs and apricots to me? Set me amid the teeth, let me dwell in the gums, so that I may destroy the blood of the teeth and chew the marrow of the gums.'

There were no toothbrushes or toothpaste; teeth were cleaned with rags and sticks. Many of the recommendations in the medical papyri are for the treatment of bad breath, which was perhaps a problem that women especially were at pains to deal with. They sweetened their breath by putting in their mouths pellets of aromatic spices mixed with honey, as, for instance:

> Dry oliban, pine seeds, terebinth resin, fragrant reed (*Calamus aromaticus*), cinnamon rind, melon, Phoenician reed. Grind finely,

mix into a solid mass and put on the fire. Add honey to it. Heat, knead, make into pellets. They will make fumigation with these pastilles. They will also put them into their mouths to make their breath pleasant.[12]

For the treatment of halitosis, the Ebers Papyrus recommends the chewing of balls of myrrh, pignon, frankincense, cinnamon and honey.[13]

It is clear from the papyri that women consulted doctors for a variety of feminine ailments. The Kahun Papyrus alone shows that these ailments included depression,[14] general aches and pains,[15] problems with menstruation,[16] threatened miscarriage,[17] injury during parturition,[18] and cancer of the womb.[19] There are three cases of what might have been venereal disease: if this is so, then it would have been gonorrhoea, which is thought to have occurred in ancient Egypt, rather than syphilis, for which there is no clear evidence.[20]

A doctor's *modus operandi* seems to have been to question his female patient closely on her symptoms and past medical history, and to observe external features such as the colour of the whites of her eyes, the state of the pupil, the texture and colour of her skin and the appearance of her breasts. Any physical examination he might make was usually external only – there is no evidence to suggest that much in the way of internal inspection was made.

One case[18] describes a woman's symptoms as being due to 'want in her womb', which has been interpreted as meaning that the woman had such an overwhelming desire to bear a child that she had become physically ill. Another[14] ascribes the woman's condition to 'disturbance of the womb'; and the depression referred to above was thought to emanate from the same source:

Instructions for a woman who wants to lie down, making no effort to get up, and being unwilling to shake it off. You should say about her: 'This is spasms of the womb.' You should treat her as follows: make her drink a pint of *haawy*-fluid and make her vomit it at once.[14]

The ancient Egyptian doctor was not the last to attribute disorders in a woman's nervous system to her womb: the very word 'hysteria' comes from the Greek *hustera*, 'womb', which was held to be the seat of the malady.

The same remedy for menstrual problems as that given in the Kahun Papyrus[16] is found in the Edwin Smith and Ebers Papyri: vaginal douches of aromatic mixtures administered so that 'the blood may be made to come away.' In cases of uterine prolapse, pessaries made of wine or beer and vegetable extracts were employed.

In one case in the Kahun Papyrus[19] the patient is said to have become ill because her womb has become 'diseased because it has moved.' It is evident from this, and from other examples, that the Egyptians believed that the pelvic organs, including the womb, were capable of wandering from their proper positions to other places within the abdominal cavity, and that if they did so, they could become diseased. Where this occurred, the straying organ had to be attracted back to its place by means of fumigations, often made of oil and frankincense, over which the patient stood. In the Kahun Papyrus, the doctor is instructed to ask the woman, 'What do you smell?' If her reply was, 'I smell burning flesh' then he was advised to prescribe for her a 'fumigation over everything she smells as burning flesh.' It is thought that the woman in this instance was suffering from cancer of the genitalia – hence the smell of burning flesh, said to be symptomatic of the disease. The doctor's treatment of the disease by tackling its symptom, a smell of burning, with another burnt odour, that in the fumigation, owes more to magic than to what would currently be regarded as medicine; and if the disease really was cancer, then the woman would have remained uncured.

Ancient Egyptian doctors were capable of recognizing when they were faced with a hopeless case. One case in the Kahun Papyrus[21] deals with a woman 'suffering in her teeth and her gums so that she is unable to open her mouth'. A fumigation is recommended, but a warning is given that other symptoms in this case indicate that she is suffering from 'an incurable disease'. In the Edwin Smith Papyrus, the diagnosis (see page 77) of a case is followed by the 'verdict'. Three verdicts were employed: 'An ailment which I will treat', for cases within the competence of the physician and for which he anticipated a successful outcome; 'An ailment with which I will contend', for difficult cases where the outcome was uncertain; and 'An ailment for which I can do nothing', for hopeless cases. It is interesting to note that hopeless cases were described with as much detail as the others, and that instructions for the nursing care of the terminally ill were given.

It is often difficult to ascertain from the papyri the exact nature of the disease that is referred to. It has been suggested that there are three cases[22] in the Kahun Papyrus which refer to venereal disease. One describes a woman 'whose eyes are diseased so that she is unable to see, and she has pains in her neck'; another describes one who is 'diseased in every limb, with painful eye-sockets'; and the third refers to a woman 'who aches in every limb and in the sockets of her eyes'. Little is known about the incidence of venereal diseases in ancient Egypt;[20] and it can be seen from the examples quoted above that information from the medical papyri is somewhat unhelpful – these three cases could, after all, be simply describing influenza.

The treatment recommended for women's ailments was not, as has already been pointed out, surgical. Instead, fumigations, either pleasant-smelling or noxious, were administered, as were pessaries and vaginal douches. Medication, often consisting of mixtures of dates and other fruits, milk, beer, oil, honey and herbs could be taken orally; and a dietary regime of certain foods, such as raw liver, cereals and even an ancient Egyptian version of muesli made up of grain and nuts in milk, was often prescribed. Honey and myrrh were used as salves for cuts and burns, evidently with some success in preventing infection and scarring.[23] A variety of drugs could be prescribed for those ailments which were not specifically related to women.

We cannot be certain how many different drugs were available to the doctors of ancient Egypt for the treatment of their patients, due largely to the imperfections in our ability to translate certain words in their vocabulary. However, enough drugs have been identified for it to be claimed on behalf of ancient Egyptian physicians that they knew and made use of at least a third of the medicinal plants found in a modern pharmacopoeia. Durra (sorghum) and cinnamon were commonly used for indigestion and digestive disorders, and saffron was used to alleviate stomach cramps and colic. Intestinal worms were curbed with pomegranate bark. Anaemia was treated with calamus which, because of its tannic acid content, was also used as a cure for dysentery. Sage was employed for inflammation of the throat. Many of these plants must have been expensive to obtain – cinnamon, for instance, was brought from India and China to Egypt by the nomadic traders of Arabia; saffron and sage came from Crete. Certain minerals had a medicinal use: salves made from copper ore, galena and charcoal were applied to inflamed eyes and solutions of lead, copper or sulphur salts were trickled into the eyes by means of goose quills. Trachoma was treated with alum or aluminous clay and copper – as it is today.

Whether the ancient Egyptians had drugs that were efficacious in general anaesthesia, as is sometimes claimed, is very doubtful. They used opium as a sedative and belladonna as a local anaesthetic; but if an ancient Egyptian doctor thought it necessary to render a person unconscious, or at least semi-conscious, prior to a surgical operation, then it is probable that the patient was given enough alcohol to drink to render him or her insensible.

Many ingredients in the medicines concocted by the ancient Egyptians seem appalling to us: human urine, child's excrement, gazelle dung, crocodile and lizard excrement, pelican and fly droppings, all examples of what has been termed 'sewerage pharmacology'. However, the modern treatment for trachoma employs aureomycin, an antibiotic which is formed from a mould; and today trichiasis, which the ancient Egyptians cured by swallowing bat's blood or urine, or applying them to the eye, is treated with vitamin A. It has been shown that bacteria which live in the human body release their excretory products into their host's faeces and urine, which become rich thereby in antibiotic substances; and that bat dung contains a great deal of vitamin A. Thus, it would seem probable that, as in many other societies, the ancient Egyptians, who originally used excrement in their magic spells as vile substances with which to drive out demons, gradually identified some substances of genuine merit.

A girl in ancient Egypt usually married shortly after beginning to menstruate (which was called her 'time of purification'), and could expect to bear her first child at about twelve to fifteen years old, thereafter producing a child per year so that women seldom had fewer than four or five children. Eighteen to twenty years was the average life span although many women lived much longer, producing more children – in modern times it has not been unusual for women of fifty to give birth. Conditions in the home, where all births took place, were such that lack of hygiene, even in upper class houses, must have led to a high rate of infant and maternal mortality from gastric disorders, diarrhoea and dysentery. In the first century AD, Celsus noted that dysentery carried off 'mostly children up to the age of ten; other ages bear it more easily. Also a pregnant woman can be swept away by such an event, and even if she herself recovers, yet she loses the child.'[24]

In contrast to the modern western world, where childbirth often seems to be regarded as an illness, the ancient Egyptians considered it to be simply a part of life. In the normal course of events, women would be advised and tended by female relatives and friends, and by the local village midwife; the pregnancy and subsequent birth would be a straightforward matter accomplished with the minimum of medical fuss. When necessary, a professional midwife would be called in; a doctor was seldom consulted during a normal birth, although a large part of a doctor's clientele consisted of women asking for help with difficulties of conception and fertility. Inevitably, complications would sometimes arise, both during pregnancy and in the course of parturition; even women of the highest social class had little hope of obstetrical assistance. The mummy of the Eleventh Dynasty princess, Hehenhit, for example, shows that she had a narrow pelvis and died shortly after delivery with a vesicovaginal fistula.[25] Many women must have died of uterine haemorrhage and puerperal sepsis. It is impossible to calculate how many, but the figures would probably bear comparison with rural England between the sixteenth and eighteenth centuries where it has been calculated that for every thousand baptisms, twenty-five mothers died.[26]

Given the importance of fertility to an ancient Egyptian woman, it is not surprising that the medical papyri contain tests to ascertain the likelihood of a woman bearing a child. The Berlin and Kahun Papyri give instructions on the examination of a woman's breasts in order to ascertain whether she will conceive: one case in the Kahun Papyrus[27] states that if the vessels (meaning veins?) of her breasts are enlarged, then she will. Most of the procedures for fertility tests, outlined in the papyri, are based on the theory that in a fertile woman there is free and unimpeded passage from her vagina to other areas of her body.

Another case[28] in the Kahun Papyrus recommends that a woman should sit over a mixture of beer and dates. If she vomits, she will conceive; if she does not vomit, she will not. The number of times she vomits indicates the number of children she will have. A similar test appears in the Berlin Papyrus:

> To ascertain whether or not a woman will have a child: the herb *bededu-ka*, powdered and soaked in the milk of a woman who has borne a son. Let the patient eat it . . . if she vomits it, she will bear a child, if she has flatulence, she will not bear.

Hippocrates, writing some fifteen hundred years later than the Kahun Papyrus, gives the same recipe:

> Take figs or the plant *butyros* and the milk of a woman who has borne a boy, and let the woman drink it. If she vomits, she will bear a child, if not, she will have no child.[29]

A similarity between Hippocrates's methods and those of ancient Egypt is also found in a case in the Kahun Papyrus,[30] where the recommendation is that a woman insert an onion into her vagina. If, next day, her breath smells of onions, she will conceive. If not, then 'she will never give birth'.

Should a woman prove to be fertile, then she was sometimes

given advice on how to conceive. The Kahun Papyrus, for example, gives a recipe for a fumigation, 'to be taken at suppertime' in order to facilitate conception.[31] And occasionally, an aphrodisiac is prescribed – a half-a-dipper-full of milk placed in the vagina, for example.[32]

A woman's preoccupation with her fertility and sexuality is perhaps an explanation for the numbers of so-called 'fertility figurines',[33] usually made of faience or clay, that have been found in houses, in shrines dedicated to Hathor, and among the grave goods not only of women, but also of men and children. These figurines used to be described as dolls or, by less delicate scholars, as 'concubines for the dead', inferring that they were put into the tomb for use in the Afterlife by the (male) tomb-owner. At first glance, the figurines, which are always of naked women, seem to be the embodiment of the erotic fantasies of at least some men. But closer inspection reveals that little attention has been paid to the modelling of breasts or faces, but that hips and buttocks are exaggerated in size, the genitalia are emphasized, with the pubic triangle often picked out with paint on faience figurines, or pricked with dots in those made of clay. There is a strong likelihood that these figurines were offered by women to ensure their own fertility; and those found among the grave goods of men were to enable the deceased to regain their sexual potency.

Once a woman believed that she had conceived, then naturally she was eager to prove as quickly as possible that she had done so. Apart from an opinion based on his observations of the condition and colour of her eyes, skin and breasts, an ancient Egyptian doctor could offer her several pregnancy tests: he could introduce into her vagina fumigations or pessaries; and he could observe the effects of samples of her urine on grain, seeds or plants.

Two papyri, Berlin and Carlsberg VIII,[7] pay special attention to tests for pregnancy. In them, a woman is asked to urinate daily on two cloth bags, one containing emmer (wheat) and the other barley. If both germinated, she was said to be pregnant; if neither did, then she was not. It has been known since 1927 that a particular hormone is present in the urine of a pregnant woman; and modern pregnancy tests are based on this fact. It is possible that ancient

Egyptian doctors first tested the effect that urine had on grain simply because they associated grain with life, and they expected that a woman who was carrying new life would have an affinity with the grain. In doing so, they would have observed what we now know to be hormonal effects, for it has been demonstrated in modern times that the urine of pregnant women can sometimes cause grain to germinate, whereas that of men and of women who are not pregnant always causes it to wither.

A pregnant woman was often given special foods to eat so that her child would be born healthy and handsome. As in other cultures, including our own, many modern Egyptians, especially the *fellahin*, believe that the health and eventual appearance of the unborn child is affected by the food his mother eats, and by the things she beholds during the pregnancy. Steps are taken by a pregnant woman to avoid unpleasant sights; but on the other hand, she will take the trouble to come into contact with pleasant objects. For example, she believes that if she looks habitually upon a beautiful face, she will bear a beautiful child. It seems probable that a pregnant woman in ancient Egypt behaved in much the same way.

Having become pregnant, the burning question in a woman's mind was often whether the child would be male or female. Two cases in the Kahun Papyrus[34] recommend an examination of a woman's abdomen and face respectively to ascertain whether the child will be a boy. The Berlin and Carlsberg Papyri, and later on Hippocrates, advocate the observation of a woman's face and of the state of her breasts to determine the sex of the child she is carrying.

A further refinement of the urine test on grain was that if the barley grew first, it was thought the child would be a boy, but that if the emmer was first to germinate, then the child would be a girl. We cannot know what the Egyptians thought of the reliability of this test, since it only has the virtue of a fifty per cent probability of being correct! In all likelihood, the ancient Egyptian doctor based his theory not on scientific observation but on the different gender of the nouns, barley and emmer: barley (*it*) is masculine, and a homonym of the word for father; and emmer (*bdt*) is feminine.

The same belief that urine could be used to ascertain the sex of the unborn child was found in seventeenth-century Europe, and was noted by Paullini:

Make two holes in the ground, throw barley into the one and wheat into the other, then pour into both the water of the pregnant woman, and cover them up again with earth. If the wheat shoots before the barley, it will be a boy, but if the barley comes up first, thou must expect a daughter.[35]

And a similar recipe is in a nineteenth-century English book called 'The experienced midwife'.

Today, it is possible to learn the sex of one's unborn child from some of the ante-natal tests that are commonly carried out. But until very recently it has been the custom, in many societies, for 'old wives' to hang a wedding ring on a piece of string and hold it above the pregnant woman's stomach, the sex of the child then being determined by the direction in which the ring rotates. The longing to know is age-old!

Inevitably, a woman would sometimes prefer not to become pregnant, for a variety of reasons such as the state of her health, or the number of children, both living and dead, that she had given birth to already. One of the reasons why an ancient Egyptian woman breast-fed her child until the age of three (in modern Egypt, peasant women often suckle their children to the age of two) was probably due to her belief, held by many women in many cultures both ancient and modern, that a lactating mother could not become pregnant. It was thus an attempt to 'space' her family.

There were, however, other more efficacious ways. The Kahun, Ebers, Berlin, Carlsberg and Ramesseum Papyri all contain prescriptions for contraceptive measures. In the Kahun Papyrus, there are three:[36] one recommends that honey and sodium carbonate (natron) be sprinkled into the vulva; another, that a substance, the name of which is indecipherable, be used in the same way. The third prescribes crocodile dung cut up in sour milk. This method is the most interesting, for crocodile dung is not unlike a sponge soaked in weak acid. A sponge soaked in vinegar was a common contraceptive device until quite recently in the Western world; and it is still used by many *fellahin* today. The Ramesseum Papyrus IV also recommends the use of crocodile dung, this time placed on moistened fibres at the opening of the uterus.

The Ebers Papyrus states that pregnancy may be prevented for 'one, two or three years' by a mixture of acacia tips, coloquintida (bitter-apple) and dates bound together by honey and placed in the vulva. Jellies in which lactic acid is the chief component are still used as spermicides in the United Kingdom and the United States.

The Berlin Papyrus gives a recipe to prevent pregnancy which prescribes fumigation of the vagina with a substance called *mìmì*. A mixture of fat, *m33tt*-herb (mandrake?), sweet ale, boiled together, is then to be swallowed by the woman on four consecutive mornings in order 'to get rid of it'. Was this a 'morning after' pill?

Many of the habits and customs of the ancient Egyptians are still to be found in Egypt today, but nowhere are they more evident than in the rituals and practices which surround the birth of a child. Until comparatively recently, a male doctor did not treat women. This custom has been, and sometimes still is, followed elsewhere in the world: in those Muslim countries where the harem system is strictly observed, religion and modesty forbid a male physician to touch, and sometimes even to look at, a woman not of his own family. He has therefore to resort to other ways of making a diagnosis of her condition: he may ask questions, which are relayed to the woman by her husband; dolls may be used as surrogates. A similar state of affairs existed in Europe in the modern era, during the transition period when the barber-surgeons were becoming doctors; and, in the prudish Victorian era, beyond that. These doctors examined a female patient as she lay under a sheet, and made their diagnosis by touch but not by sight. In Egypt, until the early part of this century, a male doctor normally had nothing to do with a pregnant woman; only if her life became endangered was he likely to be called in. Otherwise, childbirth was the province of female midwives, just as it normally was in ancient Egypt, although there it was more for reasons of economy than for those of modesty and religion.

Judging from the hieroglyphs used to express the verbs 'to give birth' and 'to deliver', in the earliest times ancient Egyptian women squatted on the ground while giving birth. Eventually, it became the custom to place a brick under each foot.[37] From these two bricks there developed a structure known as the *mshnt*, which was in use some time before 2500 BC.[38] The *mshnt* was a sort of confinement chair made of brick, which was replaced, probably at an early date, by one made of wood. Although no examples of these chairs have been found, it is probable that they resembled those that were used, especially among the *fellahin*, until comparatively recently.[39] It used to be the custom for the midwife to arrive at a confinement bringing with her the birthing stool, which was made of wood, and often highly decorated. The front of its seat was hollowed out into a semi-circle, and two upright wooden rods were affixed to each corner of the front edge for the woman to grasp for support when the time came for her to bear down during her labour.

We have no information on delivery in ancient Egypt, except that given in the Westcar Papyrus.[40] During Reddjedet's labour, Isis placed herself in front of her and Nephthys behind her, presumably supporting her; and Hekat 'hastened the birth'. In the story, Hekat would have used magic to do this; in real life, a midwife would probably have squatted in front of the woman in labour, usually making no attempt to interfere with the progress of the birth, but encouraging her until, as with Reddjedet, 'the child slid into her hands'. In modern Egypt, female relatives of a woman in labour often sit around her, groaning and shrieking in sympathy with her. So must it have been in ancient Egypt. If the course of the labour became too prolonged, a stimulant was administered, either applied externally to the lower abdomen or internally by means of pills and suppositories; and in the form of hot cordials. According to the Ebers Papyrus, many kinds of material were used: salt, honey, oil, onions, mint, incense, wine; and even ground-up scarab-beetles and tortoise-shells. Sympathetic magic was often resorted to, especially for the transfer of pain:

Say the words four times over a figurine of clay to be placed upon the forehead of a woman who is giving birth.

The Ebers Papyrus[41] gives advice on how to gauge a new-born infant's chance of living: 'If a child's first cry is *ny*, it will live; if *mb'*, it will die.' Attempts were often made to resuscitate an infant *in extremis* by making it swallow skinned mice – a belief in the healing properties of mice used to be common in rural Britain, where they were sometimes cut up and fed to children to cure a bad cough. Judging by the births described in the Westcar Papyrus, once a child was born, the midwife washed him before cutting the umbilical cord. There would have been no question of the midwife sterilizing the instrument used for this purpose; or even of ensuring that her hands were clean. Although the Edwin Smith Papyrus indicates that a decoction of willow, essentially salicylic acid, was used as a disinfectant during surgery, there is no evidence to suggest that the ancient Egyptians realized the importance of antisepsis during and after delivery. When the baby had been delivered, the mother was placed in her bed. Unless she came from the sort of family in which it was customary to employ a wet-nurse, or was unable for one reason or another to feed her own baby, then she would breast-feed the infant. The Ebers Papyrus[42] states that the goodness of a mother's milk may be ascertained by its smell. The same papyrus advises that immoderate crying in a child may be stopped by a mixture of fly-dirt and a plant called *shepen*, which was probably poppy.[43]

Some importance seems to have been attached to the placenta and the umbilical cord in ancient times, especially in the royal family. There was a priest of the royal placenta; and in the story of Horus (see page 19) we are told that the god had to retrieve his murdered father's umbilical cord, which Seth had stolen, in order to give it proper burial. Spell 17 in the *Book of the Dead* suggests that the cutting of the umbilical cord had a religious significance and was associated with ritual cleansing; the spell states that when the navel-string has been cut 'all the ill which was on me has been removed'.[44] In Egypt today, the afterbirth is often called *el-walad et-tani*, which means 'the other, or second, child'; and a peasant woman who is anxious to have another child will bury it under the threshold of her house, so that when she wishes to conceive again she steps over the buried placenta three, five or seven times (all these numbers are considered lucky), so that its spirit will enter her body and in the fullness of time become a child. This belief may have some bearing on the reason for the baby burials that Petrie found at Kahun:

> Many new-born infants were found buried in the floors of the rooms, and, strange to say, usually in boxes made for other purposes evidently, by their form. In short, unlucky babies seem to have been conveniently put out of the way by stuffing them into a toilet case or clothes box and digging a hole in the floor for them . . . I fear these discoveries do not reflect much credit on the manners and customs of the small officials of the 12 Dynasty.[45]

The babies found by Petrie were never more than a few months old; they were sometimes buried two or three to a box, and protective amulets were often found with them. Petrie reburied most of them, but none of those which he gave to museums can now be traced. There is a strong note of disapproval from Petrie at the unorthodox way in which the babies had been buried – the normal practice in dynastic Egypt was to bury the dead in cemeteries on the desert edge. But it is possible that grieving mothers in Kahun buried infants who died at a very young age in the same way as modern village women bury the placenta, and for the same reason, so that a dead infant would be reborn as a mother's next child.

In ancient Egypt, a child's name seems to have been given at birth. To the Egyptians, a name was more than just a means of individual identification: it was an essential part of a person, a living thing. Hence great care was taken to give a child a lucky name, or one that would protect him or her, or one that expressed gratitude to a god. As for the mother – it would seem that in ancient Egypt, she was considered to be unclean for a period after the birth. Reddjedet, for example, in the Westcar Papyrus,[46] had to purify herself with a fourteen-day purification.

Pregnant and newly-delivered women often sought the protection of the gods. They turned to three deities in particular: the goddess Hathor (see page 18), the especial champion and protectress of women; Taweret, a goddess depicted as a pregnant hippopotamus

Bes statue, Hathor temple, Dendera

standing upright on her hind legs; and Bes, an ugly dwarf god who was thought to protect the home in general, and to frighten away harmful demons who might threaten a new-born baby and its mother. Amulets of all kinds were used to ward off harmful spirits, but especially popular were those carved from hippopotamus ivory in the shape of curved wands and decorated with, among other things, representations of Bes and Taweret.

For many women, their appeal to the gods proved fruitless, for the lack of obstetrical knowledge and the absence of antiseptic measures undoubtedly made childbirth in ancient Egypt a hazardous and often fatal undertaking for both mother and child.

CHAPTER SIX

DRESS AND ADORNMENT

The climate of Egypt is warm and almost rainless, with daytime air temperatures, during the summer, rising to over 40 °C (over 100 °F) and, during the winter, averaging 18 °C (mid-60s °F). There is a wide difference between day and night temperatures, even in summer; and winter nights can be very chilly, although, even on the coldest of them, freezing temperatures seldom occur. The average rainfall over the country as a whole is only about 1 cm a year. Obviously, in such a climate there is no necessity, except at the coldest part of the winter, to wear heavy, warm clothing, at least during the day, although it might be expected that clothes would be worn to give some protection from the sun. The Egyptians, however, became biologically adapted to living under a hot sun. They were not, and still are not, black skinned: the Greeks called them 'the sun-baked race'; and they seem to have considered it unnecessary to protect the body from sunburn, although they guarded their heads against sunstroke.

The earliest (from about 4500 BC) food-producing settlers in the Nile Valley are known as the Badarians, so-named after the site at which their culture was first recognized. Judging by what has been found during excavations at Badarian sites, the inhabitants wore clothing made of animal skins and, even at this early date, woven textiles, in the form of short skirts, kilts and cloaks, with the occasional robe or large shirt. In some graves remnants of linen have been found, and in such a position as to suggest that turbans were worn.[1] It is probable that most women wore only the fringe around the loins that is the traditional dress in many parts of Africa. Bone needles, sometimes still with threads in the eyes, have been found but only in the graves of men, perhaps indicating that at this period it was the men who sewed the clothing.[2]

It is impossible to tell to what extent the earliest Egyptians wore clothing for other than utilitarian, that is, protective purposes: the leather cloaks, for instance, may have been worn to protect a hunter against animal teeth and claws. It is clear, however, that men wore girdles made up of several strings of beads, which perhaps is an indication that they, at least, wore clothing partly for its decorative effect. The Egyptians of the dynastic period (3100 BC onwards) wore clothing not just as covering for the body but for display and as an indication of rank – the higher the status of the wearer, the more elaborate was the dress.

From very early on, most of the clothing was made of linen. Silk was not introduced until the Ptolemaic Period; and cotton, now such an essential part of the Egyptian economy, was unknown in pharaonic Egypt. It spread westward from India, possibly reaching Egypt in the third century BC; and by the early years of the Christian era the cotton trees which grew half-wild in Nubia were being utilized. Eventually, the crop was grown at a significant level in Egypt itself, but it was not until the nineteenth century that an American long-staple variety was introduced into Egypt to provide the wherewithal for the world famous Egyptian cotton. Herodotus claimed that in Egypt it was 'contrary to religious usage to be buried in a woollen garment or to wear wool in a temple',[3] a statement that has led many people to believe that the ancient Egyptians did not wear wool. It is now realized that much more wool was used, in both domestic and funerary circumstances, than has been supposed. Wool has been found in predynastic graves; and from about 2000 BC, the Egyptians had large flocks of domesticated sheep, from which it is not unreasonable to suppose that they obtained wool to make the warm clothing, especially cloaks, that was needed from time to time.[4]

Flax, from which linen was made, was a staple winter crop in Egypt, and flax-pulling (Pl. 13) is frequently depicted in agricultural scenes in tomb-paintings and reliefs.[5] The flax was pulled up by its roots, preferably before its blue flowers had wilted so that the best fibres would be obtained. The tops were then torn off the stems by holding a large wooden comb on the ground with one foot and pulling bundles of flax through its teeth with both hands. Both men and women took part in these activities, which require some strength. The flax-seeds which fell out during the separating operations were either sown to produce the next crop, or used for medical and culinary purposes. Once the flax had been turned into tow, it was roved. This was done by women, who squatted on the ground, rolling the fibres against their thighs until a sufficient quantity had been worked together to form a rove. Since the distaff was unknown in pharaonic Egypt, the roves were then wound into balls around long spindles, which were usually made of wood or stone, less often of pottery, ready for weaving. The weaving was done on looms, the earliest of which were very simple, being made up of two horizontal wooden beams supported by four short pegs driven into the ground. They were operated by women. By the New Kingdom, the horizontal loom had been replaced by a vertical loom in which the beams holding the warp threads were fastened to an upright wooden frame; and the women weavers who had operated the horizontal looms had been replaced by men.

Despite their simple weaving techniques, the ancient Egyptians were capable of producing linen of an extremely high quality, although the weave is characteristically irregular. One example, now in the British Museum but originally from the Faiyum and dating possibly to 4000 BC, has 8–10 warp threads and 10–12 weft threads per centimetre. Early on in dynastic Egypt, the women who wove the cloth were producing textiles with 64 warp threads and 48 weft threads to a centimetre, which compare favourably with a fine modern cambric, which has 56 threads to the centimetre. A great variety of white cloth was produced, ranging from a coarse, heavy type to the very fine linen which the Greeks called *byssus*, or royal linen, and which was not generally used by ordinary mortals.

Even before the First Dynasty the Egyptians were accustomed to dyeing with vegetable substances such as indigo and madder. Henna mixed with the plant *Carthamus tinctorius* gave a yellow dye, as did safflower and iron buff; and green was made by double-dyeing with indigo and a yellow dye. Alum, which came from the oases, is thought to have been used as a mordant, although the Egyptians never dyed with great confidence. Until the Middle Kingdom, the fabrics themselves were usually plain; only in the

New Kingdom did weaves of complicated patterns come into use, and these were probably introduced from Syria.[6] The first examples of embroidery also date from this period.

It has been the supposition in modern times that, in general, women take more interest in dress and fashion than do men. In ancient Egypt, at least until the New Kingdom, it seems that this was not the case. It has been estimated that ancient Egyptian men wore over forty different types of costume: kilts of various lengths, shapes and fullness, plain shirts, pleated shirts, overshirts and cloaks, which could be made of different kinds of linen ranging from thick, heavy material to gossamer thin. In contrast, at least for the first fifteen hundred years or so of Egyptian history, women, from queen to peasant, wore a monotonous, uniform dress.

Very few examples of actual garments (Pl. 9) have survived,[7] and those that were excavated in the last century and in the early years of this have largely lain neglected in storage, the excavators finding them of little interest. What is possibly the oldest dress in the world, and certainly the earliest so far discovered in Egypt, was excavated over seventy years ago by Petrie in a First Dynasty *mastaba*-tomb at Tarkhan[8] (*c.* 2900 BC), but was rediscovered in 1977 in a bundle of rags in the Petrie Museum. It has been restored and is now on display in the Victoria and Albert Museum in London. Information as to the course of changes in fashion has to be gleaned from statues, tomb-paintings and reliefs. An invaluable source of information is provided by the Middle Kingdom custom of placing statuettes of servants (Pl. 6) in the tombs of the rich so that, in the Afterlife, the owners of the tombs would be served in the same way as they had been in this life. These statuettes, or servant statues,[9] as they are known, provide a good record of the type of clothing worn by servants; and although it must be presumed that any innovations in fashion were first worn by the mistresses, it was evidently not long before the servantmaids had adopted them for their own use.

Artistic representations of dress had perforce to lag behind actual development and in any case, tomb-paintings portray the upper classes dressed for eternity; even when the lower classes are depicted, they are shown in working dress, which may not have been the same as that worn off duty. The upper classes were, of course, the leaders of fashion, and it is in their costume that changes are first apparent. Clothing was sewn, and needles have been found, but, strangely, there are no scenes of dress-making activities in the tomb-paintings. Most garments must have been home-made, and it is assumed that women did the sewing, although sewing implements have been found in male burials.

In the Old Kingdom, a woman usually wore a straight, tight,

Queen Khamerernebty II (and husband Menkaure/Mycerinus),
schist statue showing Old Kingdom style of dress and wig

white linen slip that stretched from just below the breasts to the ankles, the breasts being covered by the shoulder-straps that held up the dress. The straps were sometimes cut into a V around the neck, and a note of colour could be added with beading on them or around the hem. This type of dress must have had at least one seam, and a hem, and the edges of the straps must either have been hemmed or overcast. There were no plackets or buttons; openings in the seams of a garment were fastened by means of string-ties. Such a close-fitting dress was difficult to get into; the tightness of the skirt would have necessitated a side- or back-slit from ankle to knee to facilitate walking. Sleeves were sometimes worn: the Tarkhan dress has accordion pleated sleeves and yoke attached to the bodice. In laundry lists, sleeves appear as separate items;[10] it seems that they were detachable and worn only during colder weather.

Women sometimes wore a thin cloak over their dresses; and in the Middle Kingdom the material of the slip was occasionally patterned; but it is not until well into the Eighteenth Dynasty that any substantial change in design occurred. The change was, in large part, due to the advent of King Tuthmosis III (1490–1436 BC) who brought about a great alteration in Egypt's external political position. He gained control of large areas of the Near East, establishing an Egyptian empire and making Egypt the richest, most powerful country in the then known world. Exotic products and new ideas flooded into Egypt from abroad; and Egyptians developed a taste for luxury foreign items. Women's dresses in the New Kingdom became elaborate. The bodice of a dress could be draped with cape sleeves, or tight-fitting with one shoulder left bare; and skirts were full. Long, wide cloaks were worn over the dresses; and a cloak could either be worn open or worn with its edges clasped together under the breast. The garments were made of diaphanous linen, gauffered or elaborately pleated. The predominant colour was white, but this was often set off by long sashes in brilliant colours.

Judging by the evidence of formal reliefs and sculptures in general, the material used in women's dresses was largely unpatterned linen. However, a hint that in real life women had a fondness

Scribe and wife, funerary papyrus showing New Kingdom style of
dress, Nineteenth Dynasty

for colourful clothing is provided by the 'paddle dolls'[11] which seem
to have been a mainly Upper Egyptian version of fertility figurines
(see page 86). Hundreds of these 'paddle dolls' have survived, no
two of which are exactly alike. The 'torso' of each doll is painted to
represent a dress that is decorated with an elaborate and brightly-
coloured pattern.

There was not much in the style of a garment to distinguish the
dress of an upper class woman from that of someone of lesser rank.
The material from which it was made, however, was a different
matter: the higher the woman's rank, the more expensive the
material; and, in the New Kingdom, the more elaborate the

Paddle doll, wood and beads, Eleventh Dynasty

pleating. Dresses were not worn for work: they were too tight, too elaborate and, perhaps, in many cases, too expensive. It is probable that except for the richest members of society, a woman owned only one 'best dress' and that this was a prized possession. When women worked, many of them obviously found it more practicable to wear only a short skirt: servant statues show women grinding corn or kneading dough bare-breasted.

Ancient Egyptian women wore their revealing dresses without much in the way of underwear: undergarments, when worn, consisted simply of triangular loincloths.[12] Judging by tomb-paintings, reliefs and statues, the ancient Egyptian ideal of feminine beauty included, among other things, a slim figure. Obviously not every Egyptian woman conformed to the ideal. Her dress, however, gave her no help in disguising imperfections: both the tight Old Kingdom style and the transparent draperies of the New Kingdom demanded, and flattered, a slim, perfectly proportioned figure in the wearer. But there was nothing in the way of corsetry to aid those not fortunate enough to possess such a figure.

Most people in ancient Egypt went barefoot for most of the time; and until the New Kingdom, when sandals became fashionable, women seem never to have worn footwear. The sandals were made with soles of leather, palm-fibre or papyrus; and were of a standard design, that is, with two straps, one passing over the instep, the other between the big toe and the rest of the toes.

From the earliest times both men and women wore wigs. The men either cut their hair short or shaved their heads, for the sake of cleanliness and to keep cool indoors. These practices necessitated the wearing of wigs outdoors as a protection against sunstroke. Women sometimes wore hairpieces to supplement their own hair; or, more often, wigs, which were worn to disguise the poor quality or quantity of the natural hair or simply for decoration. The wigs were placed over the natural hair, and in some statues it can be seen that the owner's own hair has been carefully delineated by the artist so that it peeps from under the edge of the wig at the forehead.

The style of wig varied according to period, and in shape and size followed the fashion in clothes, with those of the Old Kingdom being short and simple, and those of the New Kingdom longer, fuller and more luxurious. In the Old Kingdom the most popular style of wig was one of narrow, jaw-length ringlets, parted in the centre of the head to hang down on either side of the face. The ends were clubbed. In another popular style the hair of the wig was short and curly and followed the natural contours of the head. The jaw-length version gradually developed into a shoulder-length wig; and in the Middle Kingdom this had become the popular 'Hathor coiffure', which consisted of two long, thick rolls of hair, curled at the ends in imitation of a cow's horns – hence the name, for Hathor was a cow-goddess. The two ringlets rested on the shoulders and

Lady Werel, tomb of Ramose, Thebes, showing New Kingdom style
of wig

the wig was arranged at the sides of the face so as to leave the ears
uncovered.

In the New Kingdom, styles were more elaborate. Especially
popular was the wig with many long strands of plaited hair. The
hair could be arranged so that all of it fell down the back; or so that
it stood out from the head in a bouffant with the ends covering the
upper part of the torso at the back and the breasts at the front.
Sometimes several plaits were joined together at the ends at
intervals all round the bottom of the wig to form a fringe. In the

Amarna Period (see page 152), the 'Nubian wig', which was similar to the short, curly wig of the Old Kingdom, was in vogue.

The wearing of wigs was mostly confined to the upper classes, although female servants could sometimes afford the luxury. Some wigs were made of human hair, sometimes imported from Nubia, sometimes, one may assume, purchased from needy peasant women. Others were made of vegetable fibres, occasionally mixed with real hair. Most were made of sheep's wool, which was either black or dark brown; or from a mixture of human hair and sheep's wool. Making a wig was quite a complicated procedure, and even when a wig was made of vegetable fibre, a raw material which was much less expensive than human hair, it was an object of value. One wig in the British Museum has been examined by a professional wig-maker: it is made of human hair and, in the opinion of the expert, 'the standard of craftsmanship exhibited in the wig is as high as in the best modern wigs'.[13] Those who could afford tombs often took their wigs, carefully stored in boxes, with them into the tomb for use in the Afterlife: the British Museum wig, referred to above, was housed in a box made of reeds.

In ancient Egypt jewellery was worn by both men and women. It was not, however, worn simply for adornment or decoration but in addition as a charm to ward off evil: the earliest form of jewellery was probably an amulet worn on a thong around the neck. From predynastic times a popular amulet with women was a cowrie shell, which, since it has the appearance of a half-closed eye, was regarded as a prophylactic against the evil eye, a force still widely feared in some countries around the Mediterranean. Many women put their faith in a cowrie-shell amulet as a means of defending their children against the evil eye. During the dynastic period, the most popular amulets were probably the scarab, the Eye of Horus (𓂀) and the *ankh*, the hieroglyphic sign meaning 'life' (𓋹); closely followed by other hieroglyphic symbols: the *tyt*-sign (𓎬 -the 'girdle of Isis'), the *s3*-sign (𓎤) and the *djed*-column (𓊽). The first two amulets conferred upon the wearer good luck and protection, the last four the qualities for which the signs stood when used as symbols in hieroglyphic writing, that is, life, welfare, protection and stability respectively. The rich could afford amulets made of costly materials, and necklaces to hang them on; but even the poorest woman would have been able to obtain an amulet of sorts – not, perhaps, handmade by a craftsman, but she certainly could have picked up for herself a piece of stone worn by wind and weather into a shape resembling that of the more popular man-made amulets.

Items of jewellery have been found in the graves of the predynastic era. The earliest, from the Badarian Period (around 4500 BC), consist of bangles, made of ivory or tortoise-shell, with convex outer faces; and necklaces, bracelets, belts and girdles composed of strings of various Nile and Red Sea shells, and beads. Both women and men wore these types of jewellery. Anklets have also been found, but they seem to have been worn exclusively by women. The beads, which have uneven borings, are in simple shapes such as discs, cylinders and barrels. They were most often made from calcite, feldspar, limestone, lapis lazuli and turquoise, which, as it was quite rare at this time, was usually substituted by steatite. Copper was also used, and so was bird and animal bone, horn and ivory – hippopotamus rather than elephant. Pendants made from pebbles of diorite, porphyry, chalcedony, flint and quartz were worn on some necklaces; and on others amulets, most often in the shape of a hippopotamus or a gazelle-head. The girdles, made of small beads plus spacers, were often massive.

In the Naqada I Period (around 4000 BC), the type of jewellery worn was similar to that of the Badarian Period, except for anklets, which no longer occur. New additions were finger-rings and forehead ornaments in the shape of open hoops. The commonest materials employed to make the jewellery were steatite, rock crystal, chalcedony, carnelian, calcite and shell. There was an increase in the use of lapis lazuli and jasper, but copper was rare. A new substitute for turquoise was found – a quartzite core coated with a vitreous alkaline glaze in green or blue, evidence that the Naqada I jewel-makers were becoming adept in the manufacture of material rather than relying on what could be found occurring naturally.

In the last predynastic period, Naqada II (around 3500 BC), garnet, olivine, malachite and fluorospar were added to the repertoire of bead-making materials; and so were gold beads made from strips of metal or foil pressed over a stone core. Glazed composition beads became more common. The shapes of the beads became more regular: the most popular shape was still a cylinder, a barrel or a disc; but lenticular, tabular, conical, oblate and faceted beads were also made. The craftsmen of the period were capable of making stone beads with comparative ease, and so shells were used less often. In addition to bangles, bracelets, necklaces and girdles, anklets reappeared. Hawk, hedgehog and, for the first time, claw-shaped, amulets were popular.

By the Old Kingdom (Fourth–Sixth Dynasties, 2613–2181 BC) 'jewellery among the lower classes seems to have become almost exclusively the adornment of women and children.'[14] This was not the case among the rich; for them a new type of necklace, the broad collar (see page 108), became a regular piece of jewellery for men as well as women. It is known that elaborate articles such as inlaid bangles and funerary diadems were made for the rich, but very few examples, and even fewer masterpieces, remain. The principal form of jewellery worn by an ordinary woman of the period was a bead necklace, often decorated with an amulet as a pendant. The most popular shape for the amulet was a frog, a dog's head, a hippo-potamus or a human hand. By this time, beads were readily available to all but the very poorest women, and so shell necklaces became even less popular.

The jewel-makers of dynastic Egypt were capable of producing jewellery of great delicacy, beauty and originality of design. The oldest-known pieces are four bracelets from the Abydos tomb of King Djer of the First Dynasty, and even these early examples are of a very high quality. Unfortunately, tomb robbery from ancient times onwards means that comparatively few important finds of jewellery have been made. Nevertheless, smaller finds such as the collection of Queen Hetepheres of the Fourth Dynasty, and that of Queen Ahhotep (see page 149) of the Seventeenth Dynasty, and the spectacular discoveries at Dahshur and Lahun (Kahun) of the jewellery of the queens and princesses of the Twelfth Dynasty, not to mention the jewellery in the tomb of Tutankhamun, is enough to give us a very good idea of the art of the ancient Egyptian jewel-maker.

The ancient Egyptian jeweller knew how to smelt, mould, and

solder metal; and how to hammer it: he knew how to beat gold into incredibly thin sheets, less than one two-hundredth of a millimetre thick. He also knew how to chase, emboss and engrave metal; and how to apply gold-leaf onto other materials; and he was adept in the art of filigree work, inlay and polishing. Gold was his main medium. Egypt was able to obtain plentiful supplies of the metal from the mountains in her eastern desert, and from Nubia. The Egyptians also used two other metals, electrum and silver. Electrum, an alloy of gold and silver, occurred naturally in the Eastern Desert, and also in Punt (probably Somaliland), whence they imported it. By the New Kingdom, they were capable of producing electrum artificially. Silver was not native to Egypt and was, therefore, much more rare than gold. The Egyptians called it *ḥḏ*, or 'white gold' (not to be confused with what is now called white gold, which is an alloy of gold and either nickel or platinum), presumably because it was found in association with gold and may even have been a low grade of gold containing a very high proportion of silver. The technique of smelting silver from argentiferous lead ores was probably perfected in Western Asia, and, from the New Kingdom onwards, the Egyptians imported silver from that area in substantial quantities. It was not unknown in Egypt before that time: in the Fourth Dynasty Queen Hetepheres owned twenty bracelets made of thin shells of silver. But even in the tomb of Tutankhamun very little silver was used for the funerary equipment. Silver, therefore, had a scarcity value which made it highly prized.

Gold, electrum and silver were the metals in which the Egyptians set gemstones. They had no precious stones such as diamonds, emeralds or rubies; instead, they used semi-precious stones chosen for the richness of their colour rather than for their property of refracting light. The three favourite stones were the deep red carnelian, the blue-green turquoise and the rich blue lapis lazuli. Carnelian pebbles could be picked up with ease in the Eastern Desert. Turquoise, however, had to be mined with difficulty in the Sinai Desert, and lapis lazuli was obtained only from north-eastern Afghanistan. The Egyptians obtained it by trading with Arab camel-drivers, and lapis lazuli beads found in predynastic graves show the antiquity of the trade routes.

Other gemstones were used, either for their own properties or as cheaper substitutes for the three favourite stones. Amethyst, jasper, chalcedony, calcite, obsidian and rock crystal were sometimes employed. Amazon stone (green feldspar), found in the Eastern Desert, was used instead of turquoise; and very early on in their history, the Egyptians had found a way of making a substitute for lapis lazuli. In predynastic times, they heated shaped pieces of soapstone coated with copper ores to make a blue-green glaze. Later, they replaced the soapstone core with what was possibly mankind's first synthetic ceramic material: quartz-sand heated with soda until the sand particles fused to form a glaze; the resultant glaze green or blue coloured by the addition of varying amounts of copper. This material is known as 'Egyptian faience'; and the Egyptians eventually added glazes of red, yellow, black, white and lilac to its repertoire of colours.

These techniques and materials were put to use in the making of jewellery. The gemstones were used as inlays in gold or other metal, and as beads. The exception was amethyst, which was only ever used for beads; in the words of the art historian, Cyril Aldred, amethyst is 'a stone of a colour that has to be used with discretion and it says much for the restraint of the Egyptian jeweller that he refrained from employing it as an inlay.'[15]

Women in ancient Egypt wore jewellery in a variety of forms. They, like western women today, regularly wore necklaces (Pl. 11), bracelets and ear-rings, although finger-rings were not common. Unlike most modern western women, they wore anklets; and ornaments for their wigs. They did not wear nose-rings. The amulet on a thong developed into one on a string of beads; and then into a pendant. Chokers and neck collars of gold or faience discs were worn; as were wide necklaces which covered the tops of the shoulders. The wide necklaces, which were called broad collars, came in many patterns. Ornaments worn on the arms took the form of bracelets, which could be rigid bangles or flexible wristlets, and, from the beginning of the New Kingdom, were sometimes hinged; and solid, heavy armlets. In the Old Kingdom, it was the fashion for women to wear sets of bracelets on both forearms; but in the Eighteenth Dynasty, the vogue was to wear them in pairs on the upper arm. Armlets do not appear to have been worn before the New Kingdom, and then they were worn above the elbow. Of similar design to the bracelets were the anklets that ancient Egyptian women wore just above the ankle.

Ancient Egyptian men wore belts to hold up their kilts, but only three examples of a woman's belt are known, and since they belong to one or more of Tuthmosis III's queens, they may have been brought back by the king from one of his military campaigns in the Near East. Ancient Egyptian women may not have worn belts around their waists, but from the Middle Kingdom onwards they did wear girdles around their hips. Judging by the artistic evidence, girdles were often worn by young girls, dancers, servants and concubines as their only item of clothing, which would explain the absence of girdles in the Old Kingdom when women, even servants, were never depicted naked. Girdles have been found in the funerary equipment of one of Tuthmosis III's queens, and of the Middle Kingdom princesses buried at Dahshur and Kahun. The princesses' girdles were made of hollow gold cowrie shells, a favourite motif since the cowrie shells not only guarded the wearer but could be filled with small pieces of metal that tinkled seductively as she walked. One very fine girdle, belonging to Princess Sit-Hathor-Iunet, consists of a double row of amethyst beads, arranged in groups of ten interspersed with sixteen large gold leopard heads arranged in pairs and placed back to back, alternating with fourteen similar but smaller gold leopard heads. This girdle was complemented by a pair of amethyst bead anklets, each with a leopard's claw pendant.

The ear-ring was not common in Egypt until just before the beginning of the New Kingdom. Possibly the earliest representation in Egypt of a woman wearing ear-rings is found in a Twelfth/Thirteenth Dynasty ivory statuette of a young girl, found at Hu, near Dendera in Upper Egypt, and now in the Fitzwilliam Museum, Cambridge. The lobes of the girl's ears are pierced to take double-loop ear-rings made of silver wire. Egyptian men occasionally wore ear-rings, but they were predominantly a female fashion. The most popular ear-ring in the Eighteenth Dynasty was a large one made of hollow gold hoops arranged one within the other in decreasing sizes. During the Amarna Period, mushroom-shaped ear-studs made of faience, glass, metal or stone, were in vogue. These studs developed into ear-plugs; and by the Twenty-first Dynasty, many women were wearing large plugs in the lobes of their ears. The mummies of the women of the royal family of the time show that their ear lobes had become stringy pieces of flesh. Ear-rings were large and heavy, with shanks so thick that they had to be worn in pierced ears. Sets of sleepers have been found in which the shanks graduate in size from narrow to thick: they were presumably employed to enlarge the hole in the ear lobe gradually.

Women decorated their heads, their hair and their wigs. Queens and princesses wore diadems and crowns, the most spectacular examples of which were found in the tombs of the Twelfth Dynasty queens and princesses at Lisht, Kahun and Dahshur. Other women wore fillets on their foreheads. The most popular hair ornament seems to have been a clasp made in the form of a fish. Ornaments for the wig were often very beautiful: in the Twelfth Dynasty, Princess Seneb-tisi wore ninety-eight rosettes of beaten sheet gold spaced at intervals along the ringlets of her wig; and Princess Sit-Hathor-Iunet decorated her ringlets with many gold cylinders in two lengths. In the Eighteenth Dynasty, one of Tuthmosis III's minor queens covered her long wig with a wig-cover made of thin strings of small gold cylindrical beads, which flanked rows of gold rosettes. The rosettes were graduated in size, the largest being at the top, the smallest at the bottom of the row; and were inlaid with faience, turquoise and carnelian. The whole wig-cover weighed about two kilograms, an indication of the lengths to which an ancient Egyptian woman was prepared to go for the sake of her adornment.

Many items of jewellery were made in imitation of the garlands of flowers that the Egyptians were fond of wearing around their necks and on their heads. Although even the poorest Egyptian woman managed to acquire a lucky amulet to wear around her neck, or a few strings of faience beads, jewellery must have been so expensive that real flowers would have formed the basis of most women's adornment.

Ancient Egyptian women not only had a love of wearing fine

clothing and adorning themselves with jewellery, they also paid great attention to personal appearance. This was recognized in the medical papyri, which sometimes contain recipes for beauty treatment for the hair and skin, among other things. The literature of ancient Egypt, especially the love poems, makes it clear that men found long, sweetly-smelling hair alluring. If only to attract men, women were proud of their hair and took a great deal of trouble to achieve a good head of it. The Ebers Papyrus gives several recipes for preventing hair from falling out:

> Mix together ochre, collyrium, *ḥt*-plant, oil, gazelle dung and hippopotamus fat, and rub the mixture on the head.
> Mix crushed flax seed with an equal quantity of oil, add water from a well, and rub the mixture on the head.
> Boil a lizard in oil and rub the oil on the head.

The Ebers Papyrus also gives a recipe for the prevention of baldness:

> Rub the head with castor-oil and fat from a hippopotamus, a crocodile, a cat, a snake and an ibex.[16]

One or more of the above ingredients was sometimes replaced by a dog's leg or a donkey's hoof.[17] Alopecia was treated with fly droppings, dirt from under the fingernails, or calcined (i.e. reduced to powder by heating) hedgehog quills.

It seems that some women were not content with consulting a doctor about their own hair, but also expected him to provide them with the means to harm the precious tresses of a rival. Fried worm, or the petals of a *spt*-flower, boiled in oil and then placed on the head of the victim, was believed to cause baldness; and in the Ebers Papyrus there is a recipe specifically entitled 'To make the hair of a rival fall out', an objective which was achieved by anointing her head with 'burnt lotus leaves boiled in *bn*-oil.' Fortunately for the rival, the papyrus also gives the antitode: 'Fat from the leg of a hippopotamus mixed with burnt tortoise-shell'; but she is advised that she will have to anoint herself with the pomade 'very, very often'.[18]

The Ebers Papyrus gives a recipe for making the hair grow:

> The fruit of the *dgm* (castor-oil plant), pounded and kneaded into a lump; the woman must then put it in oil and anoint her head with it.[19]

Another, famous, remedy for making the hair grow was one that was reputed to have been made for Queen Shesh, the mother of the Sixth Dynasty king, Teti. It was:

> A leg of a female greyhound, one date-stone, the hoof of a donkey. It shall be cooked in oil in a *ḏꜣḏꜣw*-pot. Then one shall anoint well with it.[20]

Many recipes are for washes for making the hair thicker, or for strengthening it; others demonstrate that the ancient Egyptians were eager to prevent greying hair. The most effective way of strengthening hair was considered to be 'a donkey's tooth crushed in honey'; and for preventing black hair turning white, the Ebers Papyrus gives several possibilities. One is for the head to be anointed with 'the blood of a black calf that has been boiled in oil'; another is for it to be treated with an ointment made from 'the blood of the horn of a black bull, boiled in oil'. The fat of a black snake could also be used, but the most effective remedy, it was asserted, was 'the blood of a black bull that has been boiled in oil'.[21]

It was, of course, the blackness of the bull that was considered by the Egyptians to be the effective ingredient in these recipes, for they believed that it would be magically tranferred to the hair of whoever applied the ointment. In reality, it was the basic ingredient common to all of the recipes, oil, which had an effect on the hair of the user. A frequent application of oil would have added strength and lustre to an ancient Egyptian woman's hair and compensated somewhat for deficiencies in her diet and the drying and bleaching action of the sun, while a perfumed oil would have imbued it with fragrance. Surprisingly, henna does not seem to have been employed as a hair treatment, and certainly not as a method of dyeing hair red, but was confined to the staining of nails and hands. Black, or very dark brown, was the usual, and preferred, colour of an ancient Egyptian's hair, although an aberrant red-gold sometimes occurred (and still does); and, in the Fourth Dynasty, Queen Hetepheres II and other great ladies wore yellow wigs.

Egypt is a country where sand blown in from the desert permeates everything and particles of it inevitably lodge in the hair, so that even hard brushing does not dislodge all of the sand. Our grandmothers thought that brushing the hair one hundred times each night and morning helped it to grow; and they often rubbed a silk handkerchief over their coiffure to give it an extra sheen. These aids to beauty were not available to the women of ancient Egypt: there was no silk; and, as far as is known, they did not use anything resembling a hairbrush made of bristles or wires set in wood. Removing the tangles from long hair without such an implement is painful, which is possibly why many ancient Egyptian women preferred to cut their hair short and wear a wig, which could be combed without fear of inflicting pain on the wearer.

Combs made of ivory or wood were used by the ancient Egyptians: fine-toothed and long-toothed combs have been found, some dating to the predynastic period. The former must have been used to disentangle knots in the hair and to comb it smooth; the latter, which often have decoratively-carved tops, were used for holding up long hair. Wood and ivory were also used to make hairpins and bodkins, which were used for decoration and to hold hair in position.

The fact that hairdressing forms the subject of two Eleventh Dynasty reliefs indicates how important it was in the life of an ancient Egyptian woman. At Deir el-Bahri two queens of the period were buried. One of them, Kawit, is depicted on the side of her sarcophagus having an extra curl attached to her wig, or perhaps her own short, curly hair, by a maidservant. The other, Neferu, is shown in a relief on a wall of her tomb chamber being attended by her maid, Henut, who is attaching a ringlet to her mistress's coiffure. In both cases a bodkin (Pl. 12) is used to pin hair out of the way while the extra tresses are attached.

Queen Kawit at breakfast, from her sarcophagus found at Deir
el-Bahri, Eleventh Dynasty

Neferu and servant hairdressing

Further proof of the importance that ancient Egyptian women attached to their hair is furnished by two royal burials at Thebes. The mummy of Queen Tetisheri (see page 149) shows that her hair was white and scanty at death and had been interwoven with false braids to disguise a bald patch; a device that was employed by her granddaughter, Ahmose-Nefertiry (see page 150) and used later on other female mummies.[22] For these royal ladies, as well as for ancient Egyptian women of all classes, their hair must truly have been regarded as their crowning glory.

Women used cosmetics as an aid to nature. The eyes were considered especially important, and from predynastic times eye make-up was used extensively by women and also by men. The Badarians (see page 94) were the first to use eye make-up, which they made from green malachite. Malachite is an ore of copper which at that time was found in sufficient quantities in the Eastern Desert, although later on the Egyptians had to mine it in the Sinai peninsula. The malachite was ground up and mixed with resin or fat, or perhaps with the oil of the castor plant, seeds of which have been found at Badarian sites. Each person was responsible for grinding his or her own malachite. The grinding was done on palettes made of stone, usually slate, carved in Badarian times, and for a time after, into rectangular or other geometrical shapes, and later in the shape of animals such as Nile turtles, hippopotami and hartebeests, and birds. Once made up, the eye-paint was kept in small vases, usually carved in ivory, which the Badarians in particular were skilled in handling.

The green malachite eye-paint was not used merely for decoration, it also had a practical purpose. Much of the dust and sand which would otherwise have been blown into the eyes was caught on the fat and thereby prevented from doing so; and, although the ancient Egyptians would not have realized it, the green shielded the eyes from the glare of the sun by absorbing some of its harmful rays.

The malachite was used as 'eye shadow' on the lid of the eye. In dynastic Egypt both men and women used 'eye liner', which they called *sdm*, to draw a line, which they extended towards the hairline, above and below the eye. There were two colours of *sdm*, one, black,

made of stibium or 'black antimony', that is, trisulphide of antimony calcined and powdered; the other, grey, made of galena, a
lead ore which was obtained from Gebel Zeit in Upper Egypt, three
kilometres from the Red Sea, where hundreds of underground lead
sulphite mine galleries have been discovered. The black eye-paint,
which the Egyptians called *msdmt*, was evidently quite costly, since
the antimony had to be brought from the Eastern Desert. In one
famous Twelfth Dynasty tomb at Beni Hasan in Middle Egypt, the
local governor, Khnumhotep, has thought it worth recording in a
relief painted on one wall that thirty-seven 'Amu (Asiatics) visited
him with gifts of *msdmt*. In Egypt today women still outline their
eyes with antimony, which they call by its Arabic name, *kohl*. It is
used for its antiseptic qualities, but modern Egyptian women are as
aware as those of ancient Egypt that the beauty of a pair of fine dark
eyes is enhanced by drawing a thin line of *kohl* around each eye to
make it appear larger and brighter.

In ancient Egypt, eye-paint was applied with a stick or needle,
which had either a flattened or a bulbous end and was made of
wood, bone or haematite – animal hair brushes were not used. The
paint was kept in pots (Pl. 1) made of alabaster, wood, ivory or
faience, some of which were double to hold the two colours, black
and grey; and the pots, together with their needles, were kept in
leather cases.

Ancient Egyptian women do not seem to have paid much
attention to painting their lips, and lipstick does not appear to have
been used to any great extent, but in dynastic times, red ochre was
sometimes mixed with fat to make a lip-salve.

On the evidence of figurines, tattooing of the body was practised
in predynastic Egypt, especially by women, presumably as a
protection against evil spirits. By dynastic times the practice had
largely died out. The only known instances of large areas of a
woman's body being tattooed were found on several of the bodies in
a group of Eleventh Dynasty princesses found at Deir el-Bahri.[23]
This has been taken as a sign that these princesses were of Nubian
descent, since tattooing was a Nubian custom. Otherwise, the only
form of tattoo in use was the little figure of the god, Bes, tattooed on
the thigh of a dancing girl or acrobat, presumably as protection.

Not only did the women of dynastic Egypt not disfigure their skins by marking them with tattoos, but they took endless trouble to cosset them. The ideal state of a woman's skin was soft, smooth and, above all, pale, to show that she did not have to spend time working out of doors. The medical papyri give recipes for curing spots, pimples and freckles; and for removing wrinkles from the face using a paste made of finely-ground rubber from the terebinth tree, wax, fresh *bhn*-oil and grass from Cyprus. Skin was made smooth by depilation with copper tweezers; and with razors, which could be made of flint or copper: a copper razor was flat, rather like a miniature axe set into a curved wooden handle. Alternatively, bat's blood was often used as a depilatory.

The hot, dusty climate of Egypt encourages those modern, urban Egyptians, who have the facilities, to bath or shower at least once a day; and the *fellahin*, who do not have bathrooms, bathe or wash in the Nile or in a canal. Ancient Egyptians considered personal cleanliness to be extremely important, and washing must have been a common daily act in ancient times.

From the earliest times, sections of the larger houses were set aside for toilet purposes (see page 126); and the ablutions undertaken first thing in the morning, termed *ii*, that is, 'washing', were obviously so commonplace that the same word is used to denote 'breakfast'. The servant-owning classes seem to have squatted or stood in a cubicle while a servant poured water over them from a pitcher. The water was probably cold, or at most lukewarm; and its cleansing properties would be enhanced by dissolving natron, that is, native carbonate of soda, in it. Peasants, unable to afford natron, would have used a 'soap' made of ash and animal fat. Deodorants were often used. They were made from turpentine, incense and a powder, the exact nature of which is unknown; and they were often scented.

The ancient Egyptians, both men and women, were fond of anointing their bodies with scented unguents. If tomb-reliefs are to be believed, it was the custom for male and female guests at feasts to wear on their heads cones of perfumed oil in solid form which, during the course of the feast, melted in the heat and ran down over the wig or hair onto the shoulders, giving off a sweet smell which presumably helped to disguise the odours of the festal food and

drink. For their unguents, the rich used scented oils such as
olibanum and terebinth, while the poor made do with castor, olive
or almond oil. The Egyptians also used many kinds of perfume.
Some were made by pressing flowers such as lotus to extract their
essence; and one, known to the Greeks as *kyphi*, consisted of myrrh,
broom, frankincense, buckshorn and several plants foreign to
Egypt. Ancient Egyptian women were famed for their sweet scent:
according to Pliny, whenever a woman wearing Egyptian perfume
passed by, she attracted even those who were busy with their
affairs.

Toilet spoons were used to pour perfumed oils over the head and
body, or to scoop the unguent from its jar. These spoons, which
were luxury items, are usually made of wood, and sometimes of
alabaster. They are carved in fanciful ways: for example, handles
are sometimes carved in the shape of a female musician or of a
servant carrying a jar on his shoulder; the bowl can be an alabaster
shell, the handle a duck's neck curved with the beak attached to the
bowl of the spoon. A favourite motif is that of a girl swimming
behind a duck, the girl's body forming the handle of the spoon, the
duck's wings hinged so that they can be folded back to expose the
unguent in the duck's body, which forms the bowl of the spoon.

Applying make-up with accuracy requires some means of seeing
one's reflection. From early dynastic times, upper class Egyptian
women used mirrors made of polished metal – there was no

Unguent spoon, Gurob, Eighteenth Dynasty

mirror-glass until the Roman Period. Poor women, according to the texts, had to make do with looking at their reflections in water. Mirrors were usually discs of highly polished copper or bronze, set into handles made of wood, ivory, metal or faience. The handles were often decorated, or shaped like a papyrus-column or like the head of the goddess, Hathor, an apt choice of motif since she was the chief protectress of women. In the Twenty-first Dynasty, the Egyptians began to decorate the surface of the mirror itself by incising ritual scenes onto it. To guard against scratches which would mar the metal surface of a mirror, and to delay the tarnishing which would mean re-polishing, it was usually kept in a wooden or copper case, lined with linen to keep it bright.

Ointments and perfumes were kept in pots and jars. These were usually made of alabaster or faience, often banded with gold. Queen Hetepheres (see page 106) had a very fine set of gold toilet implements consisting of a four-edged knife; a flat, rectangular razor with a thin handle and one rounded end; a ewer; a flat dish; and a nail pick. Toilet items were often kept in boxes made of cedar-wood decorated with ivory and ebony. One particularly fine example, found at Thebes but now in the Metropolitan Museum in New York, dates to about 1795 BC. This box, which is some 20 cm high, has a sliding compartment in its side, which contains alabaster cosmetic jars, and a lid which lifts off to reveal a mirror. It belonged not to a woman but to a man, Kemuny. Kemuny's toilet box is not the only example of men owning such things, a clear indication that interest in dress and personal adornment was not confined solely to women in ancient Egypt.

CHAPTER SEVEN

DOMESTIC LIFE

The family was a closely-knit unit in ancient Egypt, the ideal being a husband, a wife, and children. The husband was head of the household; the wife enjoyed a large degree of personal and financial freedom; and the children were under the control of both parents. As in Egypt today a man considered himself responsible for his relatives, and elderly members of the family, or widowed or unmarried sisters, or, particularly, a widowed mother, would often swell the numbers in a household, especially that of a family's eldest son. The smooth running of the household, and the happiness of the family, depended to a large extent on the head of the house's wife. As we have seen, despite their high social status women did not compete with men in society; but in the home, in her own domain, a woman was mistress and her duty was to bring up her children and to run her household as efficiently as possible.

A married woman's status was enhanced by the bearing of children, and once married, a woman would be expected by her own family and by her in-laws to have a child as soon as possible. Mothers were highly regarded by ancient Egyptian society, and the sage, Ani, spoke convincingly about the respect with which a man should treat his mother:

Double the bread that you give to your mother. Support her as she supported you. She had a heavy responsibility in you, but she did not abandon you. When you were born at the end of your months, she still carried you around her neck; and her breast was in your mouth for three years. As you grew, your excrement was disgusting, but she was not repelled, she did not exclaim, 'What am I going to do!' She sent you to school, so that you could be taught to write, and she watched over you daily with bread and beer from her house. When you become a young man and take a wife, and settle in your own house, be mindful of how your mother brought you up. Do not give her cause to blame you so that she lifts up her hands to god for him to listen to her complaints.[1]

The esteem in which a man held his mother was often so great that in some tombs the mother of the dead owner of the tomb appears alongside his wife in statue groups. It is seldom that a father appears in this way. In the later periods of Egyptian history the genealogies of tomb-owners were inscribed on funerary stelae; and it is a man's descent on his mother's side that is usually traced – his father is less often mentioned. A man's *maternal* grandfather was considered to be his protector and patron: in the New Kingdom, for instance, a young man was sometimes given a post 'for the sake of the father of his mother'. All this did not, however, disturb the natural relationship between a son and his father – and a son, after all, was expected to be 'a staff of old age' (*mdw n i3w*, a frequently used epithet) for his aged parent.

A man's love and respect for his mother above all women, even after he is married, is still a characteristic among Egyptians. The problems that this can cause for a wife may be imagined; a point well-illustrated by a quotation from Winifred Blackman which was written over sixty years ago but is just as pertinent today. Miss Blackman was told by an Egyptian friend, in a speech reminiscent of the sage, Ani:

My wife is good, and I am pleased with her, but she must remain there [pointing downward]. My mother is up there [pointing upward]. Did she not carry me here for nine months [pressing his hands on his stomach]? Did she not endure pain to give me birth, and did she not feed me from her breast? How could I not love her? She is always first and above all with me. My wife may change and may lose her love for me. My mother is always the same; her love for me cannot change.[2]

Children were clearly regarded as a great blessing by ancient

Egyptians: they were fond of and indulgent towards them, and parents were proud of their own offspring. Even the poorest of them welcomed all the children born to them. Children joined their parents on many social occasions: tomb-paintings depict them at feasts, dressed as miniature adults, sitting quietly and always well-behaved; or on hunting expeditions in the marshes, crouched at their fathers' feet holding harpoons or throwing-sticks, or leaning over the side of the skiff to trail their fingers in the water.

Strabo observed that Egyptians raised all their children. As a Greek, he would have been surprised by this, for in his own country there was a tradition that female infants, and even sickly male babies, should be exposed on a hillside for the gods to 'take into their care'.[3] The comic poet, Posidippus, remarked that 'Everyone, even a poor man, raises a son; everyone, even a rich man, exposes a daughter.'[4] Such a practice was necessary in Greece where food was often won with difficulty from the stony ground; weak children, as extra mouths to feed, were unwanted; and daughters were not considered to be assets to a family for the not inconsiderable burden that furnishing them with a dowry would place on it. In the extremely fertile Nile Valley the situation was different as far as food was concerned, and most Egyptians could afford to bring up as many children as were born to them. In addition, the daughter of an Egyptian family was not invariably provided with a dowry. Greek families in Egypt, however, often followed their own custom in the practice of infant exposure, as for example in the case of a young widow in Alexandria who, in 8 BC, renounced any claims upon her late husband's estate: in the document of renunciation it was stated that

> although she is pregnant, she will make no claim regarding the expenses incurred in childbirth since she has been compensated for that, but she retains the right to expose the infant and to unite herself with another man.[5]

In ancient Egypt the day-to-day care of children during their infancy was the mother's responsibility; and in the larger houses, a section of the building was set aside as 'women's quarters' in which

Mother nursing her baby in a sling, from tomb of Menna, Thebes,
Eighteenth Dynasty

a mother lived with her offspring. Mothers carried their babies
around with them in a sling which held the child against its
mother's body. One of the most famous depictions of this practice
is found in the tomb of the royal scribe, Menna,[6] who lived about
1400 BC. On a wall in this tomb, a peasant woman is shown sitting
under a tree nursing her child in a sling; and the same theme is
found over seven hundred years later in the tomb of Montuemhet,[7]
the Great Steward of the God's Wife of Amun around 650 BC. A
mother seems normally to have breast-fed her child for the first
three years of its life, perhaps as a safeguard against becoming

pregnant again too soon (see page 88) but thereby inadvertently safeguarding the child by supplying it with uncontaminated food. Infancy was deemed to have ended at the age of four, when boys at least could be sent to school.

Formal education was not usually given to boys of the peasant class. It was not entirely denied to girls, although until the New Kingdom[8] it was usually only those of the upper class who received it, and sometimes, perhaps, the daughters of scribes. Each department of the government service had its own school, as did the larger temples, but they were reserved for boys. Boys appear to have been sent to school as boarders until, at the age of sixteen, most of them were apprenticed to a craft. Only those intended for the priesthood or aiming to take up posts in the civil administration received a longer, academic education. Girls were not sent away to school, and it would be true to say that boys' formal education was incomparably better than that of girls. Sometimes richer families banded together and arranged for their children's education to be undertaken by a private tutor. Royal children were taught in the palace by a tutor, and the children of nobles were often permitted to share their lessons.

At school, great emphasis was placed on honesty, humility, self-control and good manners, and on respect for parents. Discipline was strict – educational theory seems to have been based on the belief that 'a boy's ears are on his back – he listens when he is beaten'.[9] Girls, not having the benefit of schooling, must have been given their code of behaviour by their mothers, but presumably brothers home from school did not hesitate to offer themselves as examples. The most widespread system of education consisted of informal instruction at home, where boys would be taught their father's craft and girls instructed by their mothers in domestic affairs. In families with a son at school, it was a mother's responsibility to provide him with his daily rations of bread and beer.

At home, a mother went about her daily routine of looking after her household. Except in large households with servants, keeping her children occupied while she did so would have concerned her. In many cases, the women of her extended family – unmarried sisters and widowed mothers, for example – would have been available to help her. Judging by the many examples that have been excavated from tombs and from town sites,[10] the children of ancient Egypt played games and owned toys which were not unlike some of those of the present day. Babies were soothed with rattles; and older children had spinning-tops and whips and played games with balls made of wood or leather. The more fortunate children had wooden toys such as cats or crocodiles with moveable jaws, dwarfs which could be made to dance by means of pulling-strings, and, in the Graeco-Roman Period, wooden horses mounted on four wheels; poorer children made their own model hippopotami, pigs, crocodiles and monkeys out of Nile mud. Boys played with small replicas of battleaxes and girls had rag dolls or wooden dolls with moveable limbs, and miniature beds to put them in.

An ancient Egyptian housewife had the same duties as her modern counterpart. Besides looking after her children, she had to keep her home clean and her linen laundered, to prepare food and drink and to do the shopping – or rather, go to market, for there were no shops in ancient Egypt. In all but the poorest households she would have had servants to manage. In modern Egypt, as in Britain up to the Second World War, middle class families with quite low incomes nevertheless employ servants, able to do so because the wages paid to servants are extremely low. In ancient Egypt many working class households would also have had at least one servant. With or without servants, a woman would have expected her daughters to help her in the house, if only in preparation for the day on which they would have households of their own to run. A son, on the other hand, was not concerned with domestic matters: even when his father had neither the desire nor the ability to send him to school, a boy's time, when he reached an appropriate age, was spent performing tasks outside the house.

Since so much of an ancient Egyptian woman's time was spent in running, or helping to run, a house, the type of house in which she lived affected the ease with which she was able to do so. In pharaonic Egypt all houses, no matter what their size and whatever the social status of their owners, were made largely of sun-dried mud-brick. Wood was used only for columns and ceiling beams, or for reinforcing or aerating walls; stone only for door and window frames. The earliest mud-brick house consisted of a square or rectangular one-roomed structure which was used mainly as sleeping quarters for both the household and its animals – then as now Egyptian peasants lived in close proximity to their livestock. Early in the First Dynasty (*c.* 3000 BC), the floor at one end of the house was sometimes raised to provide a sleeping platform for the human occupants of the house; from this developed the custom of partitioning off the sleeping quarters of the head of the house by means first of animal skins or woven cloths and later by lattice screens. Later still, the interiors of larger houses were subdivided by mud-brick walls, which were often coated with limewash, and, in the houses of the richer members of society, decorated with painted dadoes and top borders. However, the basic early house-type persisted throughout Egyptian history in the housing of the lowest stratum of society: needless to say, such houses were dark, smelly, lice-ridden, cramped and without privacy.

Large houses generally had kitchens, which were separated from the main body of the house; but in smaller houses, the preparation and cooking of food was undertaken outside the house. Thus, some sort of awning was usually erected over the entrance to provide shade for the housewife, who would have sat under it to do her cooking, spinning and other tasks. In front of the house was a courtyard where animal fodder, and many of the animals themselves, were kept; and even in the richest households the stables and byres were not far removed from either the house or the kitchen, an arrangement which did not allow for the hygienic preparation of food.

A large house generally had a public and a private section. The former consisted largely of a reception room, in which raised daises, or *divans*, were provided for guests to sit on; and several offices. The latter comprised the master's apartments – a bedroom and perhaps a small sitting-room, guest bedrooms, storage rooms, and, in the most luxurious houses, a bathroom with a cubicle in which a bather could stand while jugs of water were poured over him or her. In the house of a man named Nakht at Amarna there was even a wooden lavatory stool, which was presumably used in conjunction with an earth closet. In the private section of the house were the women's quarters, which often included a *loggia*, a lightweight construction of reeds and matting that formed an extra room on the roof. The ancient Egyptian word commonly used to refer to the part of the house reserved for women is *ipt*, which is often translated as 'harem'. The word 'harem', however, has connotations of the voluptuous and decadent world of the Turkish harem as exemplified by the Grand Seraglio in Constantinople. There is no suggestion that the living quarters of ancient Egyptian women bore any resemblance to this, and it would perhaps be nearer the truth to translate *ipt* as 'private apartments' as opposed to the more public parts of a house where business might be enacted. The women's quarters were generally on the opposite side of the house to the guest bedrooms, and access to them could only be obtained via the master's apartments. A rich man might have found it more peaceful to have his womenfolk, especially if they had crying babies, out of earshot, but it seems that his peace of mind could be secured only if he could control their movements!

Ancient Egyptian housewives seem to have placed great emphasis on keeping their houses clean, sweet-smelling and dust- and insect-free, not easy tasks given their living conditions. In a sandy, dusty country like Egypt, it is necessary to brush out a room or a house frequently: the ancient Egyptians used brooms made of reed for the purpose, and, like their modern counterparts, sprinkled with water as they worked to keep down the dust. The medical papyri offer a variety of remedies for ridding a house of pests: to keep down insects, for example, the Ebers Papyrus recommends a good sprinkling of natron and water. The same recipe is given for driving out fleas, although sweeping out the house with charcoal mixed with powdered *bebet*-plant was reckoned to be more efficacious. The fat of an oriole was used against flies; and fat from a cat smeared on a likely target kept away mice. A piece of dried fish or natron placed at the mouth of a snake's hole was guaranteed to keep the reptile inside. The rich kept their houses sweet-smelling by fumigating them with incense made from, among other things, terebinth.

In spite of all these efforts, keeping flying insects out of the house was an impossibility for the ancient Egyptian housewife and measures had to be found to lessen the suffering they caused. Herodotus observed what they were:

The country is infested by swarms of gnats, and the people have invented various methods of dealing with them: south of the marshes they sleep at night on raised structures, which is a great benefit to them because the gnats are prevented by the wind from flying high; in the marsh-country itself, they do not have these towers, but everyone, instead, provides himself with a net, which during the day he uses for fishing, and at night fixes up round his bed, and creeps in under it before he goes to sleep. For anyone to sleep wrapped in a cloak or in linen would be useless, for the gnats would bite through them; but they do not even attempt to get through the net.[11]

The hot, dusty climate in which they lived ensured that ancient Egyptian women spent a good deal of their time keeping their households supplied with clean linen, apparently washing loin cloths and underwear more frequently than other garments. Herodotus, for one, was impressed by the fact that the Egyptians wore linen clothes 'which they make a special point of continually washing'.[12] Laundry was not washed at home but in the river or nearest canal. There was neither soap nor detergents; instead, clothes were pounded on a large stone, or trodden against pebbles in the shallows, and then laid out to dry, and bleach, in the sun. Today, village women in Egypt still wash clothes at the water's edge in the age-old way: as in so many rural cultures, washing laundry is not, and never has been, a solitary occupation but a social gathering at which gossip can be exchanged. Once dry, the freshly-laundered linen was folded carefully and stored in chests or baskets, or, in poorer households, in pots. In richer households much of the laundry was sent out to professional launderers: the professional launderers were always men.[13]

By far the largest portion of an ancient Egyptian woman's day would have been taken up with the preparation and cooking of food. It would be easy to assume, looking at the long lists of food ennumerated in the menus of funerary repasts found in Old Kingdom tombs, that the ancient Egyptians loved food and were able to enjoy unlimited supplies of it. While the former supposition may be true, the latter probably only applied to the upper classes.

Egypt was a fertile land, in normal circumstances more than capable of supporting its population; but it was, as Herodotus observed, 'the gift of the Nile', and the Nile could sometimes withhold its gift of the inundation water that watered land which would otherwise be arid. From time to time food was in critically short supply, and occasionally there were famines. The rich, with their ability to purchase what food was available, and to store supplies against the 'lean times', did not suffer as much from food shortages as the poor. Even in the best of times, however, the peasants of ancient Egypt probably lived on a frugal diet; and the peasant housewife, upon whom the responsibility for feeding her family fell, must often have been at her wit's end. She and her family would have been thankful occasionally to receive the hand-outs of food which were made so that a rich man might be able to make the proud boast, in the autobiographical statement that it was customary to have carved in a tomb, 'I gave food to the hungry'.

The basic diet for an ancient Egyptian peasant was probably similar to that of the modern *fellahin*, and consisted of bread, onions, cheese and chick-peas or beans, supplemented with fish caught in the Nile and wild birds when they could be snared. As is usual, a man, as the manual worker of the family, would be given better food, and more of it, than the rest of the household; and a woman would feed her children in preference to herself, so that a peasant woman was probably the least well-fed of all Egyptians. A peasant woman made her own bread from emmer (*Triticum dicoccum*, a kind of wheat), which she would have ground to flour with a stone pestle and mortar or between two stones. After she had made dough by adding water to the flour, she would form it into round, flat loaves and bake it, unleavened, on hot stones; or on the *outside* of a stove. The stove, which was about three feet high, conical in shape and open at the top, was made of Nile mud. A fire was lit inside it, making the exterior of the walls so hot that cakes of bread could be stuck to them until they were cooked, at which time they fell off. Today, the *fellahin* eat *ash baladi*, 'village bread', made in a similar way. Herodotus observed[14] that the peasants of the Delta made bread out of the centres of water lilies; he also noted that they cooked and ate papyrus stalks, and that some of them subsisted on a diet of gutted and sun-dried fish. Cheese was probably made in the way it is sometimes made in Egyptian villages today: milk, from a goat, a sheep or a cow, is placed in an animal-skin (usually goat) strung on a frame, and rocked back and forth to churn the milk to cheese.

A daily task for the housewife of all classes was the baking of bread (Pl. 10), for even among the rich in ancient Egypt, bread was a staple food. The most common sort was called *ta*, but according to the menus carved on the walls of Old Kingdom *mastabas*, there were at least fifteen different kinds, while by the New Kingdom, the Egyptians had over forty varieties of bread and cake. What the differences were between them is not clear to us, but they were probably differentiated by shape and size – loaves could be round, oblong, conical or flat and they could be very large, or tiny; by method of baking – in an oven or on a griddle; and by the nature of their ingredients – emmer, barley, eggs, honey, fruit, fat, butter and milk among other things. Some bread, such as the Syrian which was eaten by soldiers in the New Kingdom, was made according to foreign recipes.

The housewife was also responsible for supplying her household with beer. Pure drinking water is a luxury of modern, industrialized countries or mountainous regions. The national drink in ancient Egypt had perforce to be beer, and ancient Egyptians rich and poor, male and female, drank great quantities of it. Beer was made from barley dough, which was prepared and put into pots in the same way and at the same time as bread dough. The barley dough was part-baked and then crumbled into a large vat, where it was mixed with water and sometimes with date- or pomegranate-juice for sweetening. The mixture was left to ferment, which it did quite quickly, and then the liquid was strained from the dough into a pot which was afterwards sealed with a clay stopper. Ancient Egyptian beer had to be drunk soon after it was made, for it went flat very quickly; and in the larger households great quantities of it were made every other day. In modern times, the Nubians make a similar sort of beer, usually from barley but sometimes from wheat or millet, which they call *booza*.

There was more than one kind of beer in ancient Egypt, the

Beer-maker servant statue, Old Kingdom

favourite being black beer; and beer could be of different strengths. Strength was calculated according to how many standard measures of the liquid could be made out of one *hk3t* (a measure of capacity – 4.54 litres) of barley: for example, beer of strength 2 was stronger than beer of strength 10. According to Diodorus, Egyptian beer was not much inferior in taste, savour and strength to wine. This may or may not have been true, but the rich at least had the choice of drinking wine in preference to beer. Vines were cultivated in Egypt and several varieties of wine were made from them, but home-made wine was not included among them.

A great variety of food was available to the richer housewife. She could feed her household on meat, a luxury that peasants could not afford. Beef was the most popular dish, and mutton and goat-meat were also eaten, as was the flesh of gazelle and antelope. Pork was considered 'unclean', presumably because it 'went off' so quickly in the hot climate. Fish also could be a problem: in some districts a certain kind of fish would not be eaten because it was considered divine, whereas in other districts, which did not have the same beliefs, it would be consumed with relish. These districts, however, were likely to have their own sacred and, therefore, not eaten fish! In later times, if not before, a strict taboo forbade anyone who took part in religious rituals to eat fish. The rich could afford to observe the prohibitions on the eating of pork and fish, having plenty of other foods to eat instead; the poor, however, did not have that luxury. The wealthier housewife was able to include in her menus wild fowl and game birds, duck, especially pintail and widgeon, and teal being most popular, not to mention pigeon. The common domestic fowl was unknown in ancient Egypt until, in about 1450 BC, Tuthmosis III received a gift from Syria consisting of four strange birds 'which lay every day'; but it was not until the Graeco-Roman Period that the hen was introduced into Egypt in significant numbers.

Pulses such as lentils and chick-peas were staple to the diet of all Egyptians, as were vegetables such as lettuces, onions, cucumber and garlic. The richer housewife was able to supplement these with fruit such as dates, grapes, figs and sycamore-figs. However, many things which are grown in Egypt today – potatoes, lemons, oranges, bananas, rice, tomatoes, almonds, mangoes, peaches, for example – were unavailable to her, being introduced into Egypt only in the Graeco-Roman Period and later. Sugar, one of the staple crops of modern Egypt, was unknown to the ancient Egyptians: they, being as sweet-toothed as their modern descendants, used honey as a sweetener, and bee-keeping was an important industry. Poorer people, who could not afford domestic honey, foraged for wild honey in the desert. Olives were not successfully grown in Egypt until Ptolemaic times, but had to be imported. The ancient Egyptian housewife often used herbs such as rosemary and parsley and coriander to flavour the food she prepared, while her chief aromatic seasonings were fenugreek and cumin (pepper was not imported from India until Graeco-Roman times). She also used various seeds, such as poppy; a spice called *ty-sps* (which means 'noble indeed') which was probably cinnamon; and salt, which was obtained in the Delta.

We know very little detail of how the Egyptians cooked their food; and only four words that are certainly describing cooking: *psỉ* and *fsỉ*, which mean 'cook', although *psỉ* seems to have had the narrower meaning 'boil'; *3šr*, which means 'roast'; and *ḳfn*, which means 'bake'. A spit over an open fire was the usual method of roasting – geese were speared through the beak and neck with a stick, fish through the tail. Meat was sometimes roasted on a metal grill placed over a stone hearth. There were cooking vessels of many sizes and shapes, usually made of pottery, but sometimes of metal – copper or bronze. Clay pots and metal kettles were placed either directly onto a fire or, from the New Kingdom onwards, into clay ovens. Complicated ways of cooking did not concern a peasant housewife, who did not have the same variety of food to prepare as her richer counterpart, but the gathering of fuel was a preoccupation of both, just as it is for Third World women today. Efficient fuel was a problem for the ancient Egyptians: trees were scarce in Egypt, and firewood hard to come by. Dried reeds and straw were used, but although they blaze up when first lit, they need to be quickly and frequently replenished. Dried dung was therefore the most common domestic fuel. The rich must have cooked their large joints over charcoal, but the authorities kept strict control of its issue. Whatever fuel was used, it is clear from the tomb-reliefs that fires needed constant fanning, and at least one servant is always shown performing this task. They were lit by means of a bow-drill; and tinder would probably have been wool.

As a general rule, most Egyptians rose early – just before dawn in the case of the peasants – and went to bed shortly after nightfall, which was at about six o'clock. Breakfast was thus eaten early in the morning, and in most Egyptian households, the main meal of the day, dinner, was eaten at midday. Sometimes, a light meal was taken in late afternoon. Judging from tomb-reliefs, the head of the household ate breakfast while he was dressing; and many a noble lady partook of hers while her maidservant attended to her hair. There were no large tables around which the whole family could gather to eat; instead, richer Egyptians ate from individual, small tables and most Egyptians squatted or sat, on mats or sometimes on cushions, on the ground. The rich had a large variety of dishes, cups, bowls and plates available to hold the food; and if necessary, it was cut with a knife. Forks were unknown and spoons were probably used more often to scoop up unguent rather than food: in general, Egyptians of all classes ate with their fingers. The dirty dishes and utensils were washed and scoured (with sand) at the river's or canal's edge by the women of the household or by female servants.

On the evidence of many reliefs in tombs of all periods, the ancient Egyptians liked to indulge in leisure time activities. The poorer classes, of course, had fewer opportunities for such things, and not many peasant women would have had the time for much in the way of recreation, although even peasants could afford simple balls made of plaited reeds or straw to use in the ball-games enjoyed by young women. Rich Egyptians, however, had plenty of leisure time, and a variety of ways in which to enjoy it. Sitting in the garden, enjoying the perfume of flowers painstakingly grown there, was a favourite outdoor pursuit of both sexes, the women taking care to safeguard their complexions by keeping to the shade. Outdoor games in the form of 'hunting, shooting and fishing' were very popular, although as far as women were concerned they were spectator sports only. A sportsman was often accompanied by his family: his sons took part in the sport if they were old enough to do so, his wife and daughters stood by encouraging him and applauding his prowess.

Indoors, both male and female Egyptians enjoyed playing a variety of board games, the most popular of which was 'Senet' or 'Passing through the Underworld', a game for two players. There are scores of representations in the tombs of the Old Kingdom onwards showing Egyptians playing Senet, and it is obvious that it was a national game played by all classes, although not many peasant women numbered this or any other board game among their pastimes. Perhaps the most famous representation of the game is that depicted in a relief in the tomb of Nefertiry, in which Ramesses II's favourite queen is shown sitting alone, playing Senet.

Pet animals were popular, especially with richer Egyptians. Dogs similar to Salukis, greyhounds, basset hounds and mastiffs were known in ancient Egypt: men used them as hunting dogs, and brought them into the house, where they were allowed to sit at their master's feet. The lady of the house regarded a good housedog as essential; and he slept beside his mistress at night. The Egyptian cat seems to have been fully domesticated by about about 2100 BC, and was used both as a working cat and as a pet. In the New Kingdom, many tomb-paintings depict the master and mistress of the tomb seated on chairs, beneath one of which sits a cat. Fond as the ancient Egyptians were of cats and dogs, however, there is no depiction of one of these animals being stroked or petted by his owners. If an Egyptian wanted a pet to cuddle, then he or she chose a monkey, which since it had to be imported from what is now Sudan or Ethiopia, and fed, was expensive and therefore a pet of the rich. Women in particular were fond of monkeys: many a Theban lady has been depicted in her tomb with a little monkey seated under her chair chewing a piece of fruit, a leash around its neck (Pl. 7); and in her daily life, her favourite cosmetic jar or spoon is likely to have been carved with the representation of a baboon, the sacred animal of the god of wisdom and writing, Thoth. Thoth was also the god of time, and it may be that by decorating her cosmetic implements with his image, a woman was endeavouring to keep his ravages at bay!

It seems clear from numerous tomb-reliefs, especially those dating to the New Kingdom, that ancient Egyptians of the tomb-owning classes enjoyed entertaining large groups of relatives and friends at banquets. The responsibility for preparing for the banquet would have fallen largely on the lady of the house, who would have supervised the thorough cleaning of her house and seen to it that large amounts of bread and beer had been made, that many jars of wine had been cooled and that a variety of meat, fowl and other foodstuffs had been cooked. She would have taken the 'best crockery' out of storage – painted pottery plates, alabaster bowls, perhaps even some cups of gold and silver. She might have

arranged flowers around the house with her own hands; and she
would have made certain that garlands of flowers were ready to
place around the necks of guests as they arrived. Cones of perfumed
wax would have been prepared to place on the head of each guest.

During the banquet, men and women ate in the same room, and
servants – in the New Kingdom, usually young, lissom girls wearing
nothing but a girdle around their hips – plied them with food and
drink, and renewed the wax cones as they melted in the heat. Both
during the banquet and after it, the party was entertained by
musicians, dancers and acrobats, who, in the New Kingdom
especially, were nearly all female (see page 47). And the wine and
the beer were kept flowing. The ancient Egyptians seem to have
believed that at banquets they should drink in order to become
intoxicated; and in one Eighteenth Dynasty relief, a servant's
exhortation to 'Drink this, my lady, and get drunk', elicited the
enthusiastic reply, 'I shall love to be drunk'. It seems that all
ancient Egyptians felt that there was no disgrace in drunkenness. In
this respect if not truly in any other, there was in ancient Egypt
equality between the sexes!

CHAPTER EIGHT

WOMEN OF POWER

The women whose lives have been fleshed out in the preceding chapters of this book have largely been the 'little people' of history. Most of these women exercised little power outside the domestic sphere, took no part in political affairs and had little influence on the course of Egyptian history. There were women of power in Egypt, however; royal ladies whose deeds have been preserved in official records and documents, and who have left behind the enduring evidence of their monuments.

There were few women among the rulers whose exploits make up the official history of Egypt, a fact well-demonstrated in the *Aegyptiaca* which was written, in Greek, in the third century BC by the Egyptian scholar-priest, Manetho. Only fragments of this work survive, mostly in the form of transcriptions or résumés by later writers – for example, the Christian chronographer, Julius Africanus (*c*. AD 220) – but it is clear that Manetho's original work consisted basically of lists of royal names arranged into groups called 'dynasties', beginning with the First Dynasty (*c*. 3100 BC) and ending with the Thirtieth Dynasty (343 BC). Of over five hundred rulers in Manetho's list, only four are women.

Modern historians have adopted Manetho's dynasties, and divided them into groups known as the Old, Middle and New Kingdoms, each of which represents an historical period during which a strong central authority was in control of the whole of Egypt. The years between the Old and Middle Kingdoms and the Middle and New Kingdoms are known as 'Intermediate Periods' and were times of political confusion. It is evident that the ancient Egyptians were more comfortable when the strong central authority was exercised by a male, the king who from the beginning of Egyptian history was accepted as being divine, the earthly embodiment of the god, Horus. However, the fact that the ruler of Egypt was identified with a male deity does not seem to have been an insuperable barrier to the accession of a queen who ruled in her own right; and according to Africanus, in the reign of King Binothris in the Second Dynasty 'it was decided that women might hold the kingly office.' In spite of this, it was not until the end of the Sixth Dynasty that a queen regnant appeared upon the throne of Egypt.

The first Queen Regnant of Egypt was Nitocris (*c*. 2180 BC), of whom nothing much is known except that she came to the throne at a time of political instability on the death of an aged king, Pepi II, who had reigned for over ninety years. Manetho asserted that she was 'the noblest and loveliest of the women of her time, of fair complexion'; and, according to Herodotus, she committed suicide after taking vengeance on the men who had murdered her brother in order to put her on the throne.[1] With the death of Nitocris, the Old Kingdom came to an end. It was nearly four hundred years, around 1790 BC, before another queen regnant came to the throne: she was Sobekneferu. She had been associated on the throne with King Amenemhat III, who was presumably her father; and there is evidence that King Amenemhat IV had likewise been associated with Amenemhat III. But there is no evidence of any association between Amenemhat IV and Sobekneferu, which has been taken to mean that there was a family feud from which Sobekneferu emerged victorious.[2] Sobekneferu was the last ruler of the Twelfth Dynasty, and she, like Nitocris, brought an era to a close, for after she had reigned for only three years, her dynasty, the peak of the Middle Kingdom, came to an end.

The third Queen Regnant of Egypt was Hatshepsut, who came to the throne in 1490 BC, when the kings of the Eighteenth Dynasty, the first and in many ways the most flourishing of the three dynasties that make up the New Kingdom, had ruled successfully over a united Egypt for over sixty years. It is tempting to think that when she came to the throne, some people may have been alarmed by the thought that, like Nitocris and Sobekneferu, Hatshepsut was about to bring a successful era to an end, for on past experience queens regnant had heralded a period of instability. Fortunately, the opposite proved to be the case. Hatshepsut was the daughter of one king and the wife of another, who was, in fact, also her half-brother and who had legitimized his claim to the throne by marrying her. When Hatshepsut's husband died, his son, born to him of a secondary wife, became king – Tuthmosis III. Tuthmosis was only a child at the time of his accession and so Hatshepsut became his regent, a position she soon discarded in favour of becoming queen regnant or, as she termed it, Female King of Egypt. Tuthmosis was relegated to the background.

Hatshepsut's move was a daring one, but she was in a strong position, both because of her birth and because she had the support of a powerful group of men, chief among them the Vizier, Ahmose, and several members of the priesthood of the state god, Amun, including the high priest, Hapusoneb. Her greatest ally, and perhaps the key to her success, was her chief steward, Senenmut, who had been appointed to his post by Hatshepsut's husband, Tuthmosis II. Senenmut was of undistinguished birth, his father being recorded in his tomb as simply 'the worthy', and his mother as 'lady of the house', but was clearly a very shrewd man and a brilliant administrator. He became Overseer of the Granary of Amun at Karnak and chief steward of Hatshepsut's daughter, Neferure; and added one title to another until he had accumulated some twenty offices of state. On being made High Steward of Amun, he handed over his position as Neferure's steward to Senmen, another loyal follower of Hatshepsut. There is no suggestion that Hatshepsut was in any way the puppet of these men, but it seems clear that she had the wisdom to surround herself with men of talent to carry out her wishes.

Hatshepsut's immediate predecessors had been warriors. As a woman she could not hope to emulate them, and so she concentrated on the arts of peace rather than those of war, displaying a breadth of vision in her undertakings. In Hatshepsut's reign, new monuments were built in honour of Amun and existing monuments embellished, most spectacularly by the erection of the granite obelisks, in his temple at Karnak, which she commissioned Senenmut to bring to Thebes (Luxor) from Aswan, some 200 miles away. She sent a trading expedition, led by Senenmut, down the Red Sea to Punt (probably Somaliland), whence they brought back, among other things, incense trees for planting in the garden of her mortuary temple at Deir el-Bahri (West Bank at Luxor). In this building, which was one of the most unusual and beautiful temples in Egypt, Hatshepsut intended that offerings should be made for ever, so that she might enjoy living in the Afterlife for eternity: it was probably designed by the ubiquitous Senenmut. Some of the reliefs and inscriptions in the temple are propaganda justifying Hatshepsut's seizure of the throne, for they record her divine birth as the child of Amun and Queen Ahmose. She also constructed a large tomb in the Valley of the Kings in which she intended to rebury her earthly father, Tuthmosis I, so that they might rest in it together.

In her statues (Pl. 3), Hatshepsut wore male attire – a kilt – and the *nemes*-headcloth and false beard that were the symbols of royalty. This should not be taken to indicate that she thought of herself as a man; her figure and face remain female, she is depicted with breasts. It is simply that the royal regalia was designed for a man, the presence of a female on the throne of Egypt being almost unheard of.

Hatshepsut governed Egypt for twenty-two years. She must have ruled her country well, enhancing and maintaining its prosperity, otherwise at the end of her reign the administration would not have been working so smoothly that Tuthmosis III, who repossessed the throne, was able to launch himself almost immediately into campaigns of conquest in the Near East, where he successfully established an Egyptian empire.

The fourth queen regnant was Twosret of the Nineteenth Dynasty. She was the royal heiress who gave legitimacy to her husband, King Seti II (1216–1210 BC). On his death, a boy named Siptah, whose parentage is not known, was set on the throne by Twosret and the Chancellor of Egypt, Bay; but after only six years, Siptah died, and Twosret ascended the throne herself as queen regnant. Nothing is known of her reign, but she, like Hatshepsut before her, was buried in a royal tomb in the Valley of the Kings.

The last dynasty recorded by Manetho, the Thirtieth, ended in 343 BC, after which Egypt came under Persian rule until 332 BC, when Alexander the Great added the country to his empire. The last dynasty of kings to rule Egypt were the descendants of Ptolemy Lagides, Alexander's general, who claimed the throne of Egypt for himself in 304 BC. They were not Egyptian but Macedonian Greek and might have been expected to act according to the rules and customs of their own culture which were different from those of pharaonic Egypt. On occasion, however, they chose to ignore them and conform to Egyptian custom, notably in the matter of brother-sister marriages. They have been described as 'virile if not specially virtuous rulers'[3] and had a propensity for murdering each other, an activity in which the ladies of the dynasty, all called Berenike, Arsinoe or Cleopatra, were prepared to match the men. The queens of the Ptolemaic dynasty benefited from the fact that they and their husbands ruled in Egypt, a country over which, on occasion, queens before them had exerted considerable influence.

The most famous of the Ptolemies, the last Queen Regnant of Egypt, was the 'serpent of Old Nile', Cleopatra VII, who beguiled both Julius Caesar and Mark Antony and has fascinated succeeding generations. The mundane facts of her life are that she was born in 69 BC, daughter of Ptolemy XII Auletes and his sister, Cleopatra VI Tryphaena. When she was eleven years old, her father was expelled from Egypt by the Alexandrians who blamed him for the loss of Cyprus to Rome. Berenike, her eldest sister, was instated on the throne in his place, but when three years later, with the aid of the Romans, Auletes reclaimed his throne, Berenike was executed on her father's orders. On the death of Auletes in 51 BC, Cleopatra, aged seventeen, was placed on the throne with her ten-year-old brother, Ptolemy XIII. In 48 BC, she married him; and a year later she married her other brother, also called Ptolemy, then a boy of twelve.

Shortly after Cleopatra came to the throne, Julius Caesar arrived in Egypt. It is difficult to accept that such a man, mature in years and experience, a warrior and a statesman, could have been seduced by the young queen, but they did form a union that was not only sexual but political, economic and military. They did not marry but had a son, Caesarion, in 47 BC; and by the autumn of 46 BC Cleopatra had followed Caesar to Rome, where, a short time before, her sister, Arsinoe, had been forced to walk in Caesar's triumph. When Caesar was assassinated in 44 BC, Cleopatra fled back to Egypt.

After Caesar's death, his nephew, Octavianus, formed a triumvirate with Lepidus and Mark Antony; but after the Battle of Philippi in 42 BC, Octavianus took control of the West and Antony of the East. In need of money, Antony set about plundering the cities of Asia Minor. In the field he was a brilliant commander, but in administrative matters he was lazy and easily distracted. His army loved him, even though he made rash promises about pay that he never kept. He was extravagant, always in debt, a lover of wine,

Drawing of Cleopatra: School of Michelangelo

women and song. He liked adulation, and, after Philippi, waited for Cleopatra to add her congratulations to those offered by others. When they did not come, he imperiously demanded that she come to Tarsus to give an account of herself. She did so in a way that has been immortalized by Shakespeare:

> The barge she sat in, like a burnished throne,
> Burned on the water: the poop was beaten gold;
> Purple the sails, and so perfumed that
> The winds were love-sick with them; the oars were silver,
> Which to the tune of flutes kept stroke, and made
> The water which they beat to follow faster,
> As amorous of their strokes. For her own person,
> It beggared all description: she did lie
> In her pavilion – cloth-of-gold of tissue –
> O'er picturing that Venus where we see
> The fancy out-work nature: on each side her
> Stood pretty dimpled boys, like smiling Cupids,
> With divers-coloured fans, whose wind did seem
> To glow the delicate cheeks which they did cool,
> And what they undid did.[4]

That evening, Cleopatra invited Antony to supper on her barge – an astute move, ensuring that her first meeting with him would be on what was technically Egyptian soil. Thus she established her dominance over Antony. At the time of their meeting she was an exotically attractive woman of twenty-eight, he a bluff, middle-aged soldier of forty-two, inexperienced in the ways of sophisticated women. He could never have met anyone like Cleopatra, and it was inevitable that he should fall under her spell.

For the last eleven years of his life Antony lived most of the time in Egypt with Cleopatra, bigamously married to her and ignoring his first wife, Fulvia, in Rome; and later his second wife, Octavia, the sister of Octavianus with whom he made a dynastic marriage in 40 BC. That same year, Cleopatra bore him twins, Alexander Helios and Cleopatra Selene; and five years later she bore him another son, Ptolemy Philadelphus. Antony and Cleopatra had great ambitions

Cleopatra and Caesarion, rear wall of Hathor temple, Dendera

for their children, intending to set up an empire for them. Inevitably, this brought them into conflict with Rome, and in 31 BC, they fought Octavianus and lost to him in a sea battle off the Ionian coast of Greece – Actium.

The Battle of Actium was a sea battle that Antony had no wish to fight, preferring to meet Octavianus on land; it was at Cleopatra's insistence that he undertook it. Antony's fleet formed four squadrons parallel to the shore and rather close to it. Three squadrons formed the front line; the fourth was the Egyptian, consisting of sixty ships under Cleopatra. It took up position in the rear as reserve. Soon after the fight started, thought to be an hour after noon, a fresh afternoon sea breeze sprang up – something that was known to happen often in the Ambracian Gulf. While the outcome of the battle was not yet decided, Cleopatra's squadron made sail, charged through the centre of both lines and made off. Antony boarded a light craft and followed.

Cleopatra has often been condemned for her action, and blamed for the loss of the battle. Dion Cassius, managing to be both sexist and racist, wrote:

True to her nature as a woman and an Egyptian, tortured by suspense and fearful of either outcome, she turned to flight herself and raised the signal for others.

However, another interpretation of her action is possible: perhaps Cleopatra's charge was made according to a plan agreed with Antony beforehand and was, in fact, a bid for victory:

Under oars, her heavy ships could not move fast enough to ram their lively opponents, but charging under sail with a free wind every Egyptian had one chance to sink an enemy.[5]

The ploy failed; and once to leeward of the battle, Cleopatra could not manoeuvre round to re-engage. Antony intended to live to fight another day and meant his ships to break off battle and follow him but they were unable to do so because they were under attack. Neither Antony nor Cleopatra lived for much longer: they both committed suicide, she rather more painlessly than he, for he fell upon his sword but lived for many hours afterwards. She, it is said, chose to die by the bite of an asp, probably a cobra, symbol of the goddess Edjo, who protected Lower Egypt.

Cleopatra has continued to beguile many generations. The titles of books written about her in our own time give some idea of the way in which she has exercised the imagination: *Cleopatra of Egypt: Antiquity's Queen of Romance*;[6] *Cleopatra: a study in politics and propaganda*;[7] *Cleopatra: a royal voluptuary*.[8] Her story was the inspiration for Shakespeare's *Antony and Cleopatra* and Dryden's *All for Love*; and on the English stage the role of Cleopatra has been played by actresses as diverse as Lily Langtry, Edith Evans, Vivien Leigh, Peggy Ashcroft, Glenda Jackson, Janet Suzman, Judy Dench and Diana Rigg. On film she has been played most notably by Theda Bara, Claudette Colbert and Elizabeth Taylor. And who can forget the kittenish Cleopatra of Vivien Leigh in the film of Shaw's *Caesar and Cleopatra*; or indeed the Amanda Barrie version of Egypt's most famous queen in *Carry On Cleo*! The Cleopatra of drama is indeed a lady of 'infinite variety'.

In popular opinion, Cleopatra was a beautiful and fascinating

Cleopatra, contemporary head

woman who enthralled men with her intelligence, wit and charm;
but who also had a cruel side to her nature, testing out poisons on
prisoners. Contemporary evidence, however, gives the lie to her
beauty: judging from her portraits on coins and on two portrait
heads[9] thought to be of Cleopatra, the only two extant, she had a
prominent fleshy nose and lips. According to Plutarch she was not
incomparably beautiful and it could not be said that nobody could
see her and not be struck by her beauty. He did, however, confirm
her intelligence, recording that she spoke many languages, which
enabled her to speak without interpreters to 'Aethiopians, Troglo-
dytes, Hebrews, Arabians, Syrians, Medes and Parthians'.

Cleopatra, coin, 50 BC

It is to Plutarch that we owe an explanation of Cleopatra's fascination, although it must be remembered that he was writing in the second century AD and had no personal experience of her:

The contact of her presence, if you lived with her, was irresistible; the attraction of her person, joining with the charm of her conversation, and the character that attended all she said or did, was something bewitching. It was a pleasure merely to hear the sound of her voice, with which, like an instrument of many strings, she could pass from one language to another.[10]

One of the languages Cleopatra could pass from was Egyptian, something which added to her popularity with her Egyptian subjects, for she was the only one of her dynasty to take the trouble to learn the language of the country over which it ruled.

Although only four women reigned as queens regnant throughout the whole period of pharaonic Egypt, the queen who was the chief wife of the king enjoyed a position of great power and authority. The king might have several wives, both Egyptian and non-Egyptian, most of them married not for love but for reasons of state – as a means of conferring honour on a noble family, for example, or, in the case of foreign princesses, married in order to cement alliances. In addition the king had concubines. His chief wife, however, the 'Great Royal Wife', was a woman of importance. Since descent was traced through the female line (see page 23), she was usually the daughter of the preceding king by his chief wife, the royal heiress through whom her husband gained his right to the throne. She was considered to be the daughter of a god and the wife of a god. Her children were usually heirs to the throne: her eldest daughter succeeded her mother as the royal heiress; and her son, if she had one, was crown prince, who would, when he became king, make her also the mother of a god.

In the Old Kingdom the 'Great Royal Wife' was called *sm3wt nbwy*, 'She-who-unites-the-Two-Lords' (i.e. Seth and Horus, the patron deities of Upper and Lower Egypt); *m33t Ḥr Stḫ*, 'She-who-beholds-Horus-and-Seth'; and *mwt msw niswt*, 'Mother of the King's Children'. From the Fourth Dynasty, the 'Great Royal Wives' were the only people, apart from the king himself, to be granted the privilege of burial in pyramids, although the queens' pyramids were considerably smaller than those of their royal husbands. One queen, Khentkawes, the mother of the first two kings of the Fifth Dynasty, was buried at Giza in a sarcophagus-shaped tomb that is so large that archaeologists at one time thought that it was the unfinished pyramid of a king. The tomb, which lies a little way to the west of the Sphinx, is cut from the surrounding rock and surmounted with a rectangular structure made from limestone blocks. In the south-east corner of this is a chapel from which a descending corridor leads to the burial chamber and other rooms. The whole complex is apparently unique.

In the New Kingdom the king's chief wife was called *ḥmt nṯr*, 'The Wife of the God'; *mwt nṯr*, 'The Mother of the God'; *ḥmt nsw wrt*, 'The Great Royal Wife'; and her name was written inside a cartouche, ⊂⊐ , just as the king's own name was. The influence of the 'Great Royal Wife' in the New Kingdom was unsurpassed, and this pre-eminence began with three remarkable queens of the late Seventeenth and early Eighteenth Dynasties. From about 1670 to 1550 BC a large part of northern Egypt was ruled by a dynasty of foreign kings, now known as the Hyksos. Eventually, the Hyksos were overthrown and driven out, a process begun by Seqenenre Tao I, who was a member of an Upper Egyptian family designated by Manetho as the Seventeenth Dynasty; and completed by his son, Seqenenre Tao II, and grandsons, Kamose, and Ahmose, the founder of the Eighteenth Dynasty. It is clear from such contemporary records as exist that the chief queens of three of these kings played a remarkable part in the struggle. The queens were Tetisheri, the wife of Seqenenre Tao I, mother of Tao II and grandmother of Kamose and Ahmose; Ahhotep, the wife of Tao II; and Ahmose-Nefertiry, the wife of Ahmose.

Tetisheri was the daughter of commoners and was the mother not only of Seqenenre Tao II but also of his wife, Ahhotep. Tetisheri outlived her husband, son and grandson, Kamose, and died during the reign of another grandson, King Ahmose, who paid conspicuous attention to the commemoration of his grandmother, the founder, on both male and female sides, of his dynasty. In her chapel at Abydos he recorded that in addition to the tomb and the cenotaph already built for her in Thebes and Abydos, he wished to honour her memory further by erecting a pyramid and a chapel at Abydos complete with a pool and trees, an estate and both priestly and secular staff.[11]

Tetisheri's daughter, Ahhotep, was principal lady of Egypt in the early part of the reign of her own son Ahmose. It seems clear from an inscription on Ahmose's great stele at Karnak that she played an unusually active part in her family's struggle to establish firm control over Egypt: 'she is one who looks after Egypt. She has cared for her soldiers, she has guarded her, she has brought back her fugitives and gathered up her deserters, she has pacified Upper Egypt and expelled her rebels'.[12] On her death her tomb was lavishly equipped with precious objects, including a necklace of three gold flies on a chain: the so-called Order of the Golden Fly, which was a military decoration given for valour.

Ahmose-Nefertiry, the wife of Ahmose, was probably the daughter of his brother, Kamose, and therefore also her husband's niece. Like Tetisheri and Ahhotep before her, she exerted considerable influence during her husband's reign; but she also lived on into the reign of her son, Amenhotep I, remaining the principal lady of Egypt, and eventually sharing a mortuary temple and possibly a tomb with him. After her death, her fame was greater than that of her two predecessors; and she was particularly venerated by the artisans who worked on the royal tombs at Thebes. She and Amenhotep I became the patron deities of the people of Deir el-Medina (see page 7) who prayed to the queen and her son in times of trouble.

Tetisheri, Ahhotep and Ahmose-Nefertiry set a pattern of female authority that was to be followed later in the Eighteenth Dynasty by

Queen Tiy, yew wood head

another two remarkable women, neither of whom had royal parentage. The first of these was Tiy, the 'Great Royal Wife' of Amenhotep III (1402–1364 BC). She was the daughter of the High Priest
of Min, Yuya, and his wife, Tuyu, and her marriage with the king
was arranged when she was probably eleven or twelve years old and
he was fifteen. It could hardly have been a love match, but it is
obvious that the king held a great affection for her throughout his
life. In reliefs, she is often represented with him side by side and
equal in size – in Egyptian artistic convention an indication that she
was of equal importance. Tiy advised her husband on matters of
state, a fact that was recognized by one of Egypt's allies, King
Tushratta of Mitanni (the land that lay between the Tigris and the
Euphrates), who wrote to her after Amenhotep III's death request-
ing that Egypt's good relations with Mitanni be maintained.[13]

A number of foreign princesses were also married to Amenhotep
III: in the tenth year of his reign, Gilukhepa, the daughter of King
Shuttarna of Mitanni, became his wife, arriving in Egypt with a
retinue of 317 ladies and attendants; and towards the end of his
reign, he married the daughters of two other Near Eastern poten-
tates: King Tarkhundaradu of Arzawa and King Kadashman-Enlil
of Babylon. Amenhotep III had previously married the sister of
Kadashman-Enlil and, just before his death, he requested that King
Tushratta of Mitanni send his daughter, Tadukhepa, to join her
aunt, Gilukhepa, as his wife. It seems that Tadukhepa arrived too
late to marry Amenhotep III, and instead became the wife of his
son, Amenhotep IV. None of the foreign princesses became the
'Great Royal Wife' of Amenhotep III, a position that Tiy alone
enjoyed until sometime around the thirty-first year of his reign
when he also made their daughter, Sitamun, his 'Great Royal Wife'.

Amenhotep IV, the son of Tiy and Amenhotep III, emulated his
father in making a commoner his 'Great Royal Wife'. She was
probably Tiy's niece and like her aunt exerted a great deal of
influence over her husband. Her face, thanks to the beautiful
portrait head of her that is now in the West Berlin Museum, is one
of the best known from the ancient world: her name was Nefertiti
and she was perhaps an even more remarkable woman than her
mother-in-law, Tiy. Nefertiti lived during what is now known as the

Nefertiti, quartzite head

Amarna Period, so called after the modern name of the city which her husband built in honour of the god he favoured above all the other gods of Egypt, the Aten. It was a period unique in Egyptian history, a fact that might explain why Nefertiti was allowed to undertake a role so different from that of other royal wives.

Towards the end of Amenhotep III's reign, a new power, the Hittites, who inhabited part of what is now called Turkey, was threatening Egypt's possessions in the Near East. It required a king of Tuthmosis III's mettle to counter them; but Amenhotep III was not such a king. His son, Amenhotep IV, was even less inclined to take military action, and promoted the worship of the Aten, not so much in the spirit of religious revolution as to distract attention

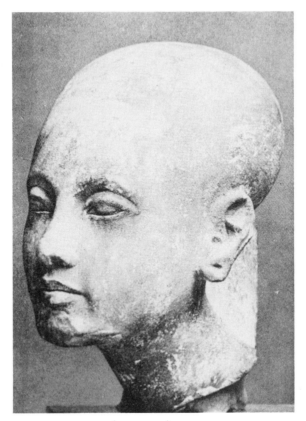

Amarna princess

away from what was happening abroad. In addition, he used his
new religion to counter the power of the priesthood of Amun. The
cult of Amun had benefited enormously from the wealth obtained
from the empire established by Tuthmosis III, who had reason to be
grateful to its priests for their support, and it had grown inordin-
ately powerful. Amenhotep IV introduced the Aten as a rival to
Amun. In the fifth year of his reign, Amenhotep IV changed his
name to Akhenaten, and three years later moved his court to the
new city of the Aten, Akhetaten (The Horizon of the Aten). There
he lived until his death nine years later: but even before he died, he
had begun to soften his attitude to Amun, sending his daughter and
her husband as emissaries to Thebes.

The Aten of Akhenaten was represented in reliefs as the sun's disc from which rays descended, each ray ending in a hand, with some of the hands holding the *ankh*, the hieroglyphic sign meaning 'life'. There was no cult image of the god; instead the king himself was the living Aten. The queen, Nefertiti, was the female element, and she played an important role in the worship of the Aten. In ancient Egyptian religious ritual, it was only the king who was ever depicted on temple walls making offerings to the gods. In the temple of the Aten at Karnak, Nefertiti is sometimes shown making the offerings, a significant departure from normal practice.[14]

Nefertiti and Akhenaten had six daughters, the first of whom, Meritaten, was married to her father after Nefertiti's death and subsequently passed on to his brother, Smenkare, who was to succeed him as king. Akhenaten then married his third daughter, Ankhesenpaaten, but when Meritaten died, it was Ankhesenpaaten's turn to be passed on to Smenkare. After the deaths of Akhenaten and Smenkare, Ankhesenpaaten married Tutankhamun who, like Smenkare, was her father's brother. Tutankhamun reigned for ten years before dying without issue. The widowed queen, now called Ankhesenamun, sent a letter to Suppiluliumash, King of the Hittites, begging him to send one of his sons to Egypt to marry her and become King of Egypt. A distrustful Suppiluliumash delayed too long in making up his mind, and when at last his son, Zananzash, set out for Egypt, the prince was ambushed and killed on his way there. Ankhesenamun was forced to marry Ay, the brother of her grandmother, Queen Tiy, thereby enabling him to become King of Egypt; after which the unfortunate Ankhesenamun disappeared from the records. The last king of the Eighteenth Dynasty, Horemheb (1343–1315 BC), who was an army officer before ascending the throne, seems to have legalized his claim to the crown by marrying Mutnodjmet, who was probably the sister of Nefertiti. Mutnodjmet and Nefertiti are thought to have been the daughters of Ay; and, since Ay had been King of Egypt, Mutnodjmet could be regarded as the royal heiress.

Most of the queens of the subsequent dynasties are known only as objects of the devotion of the kings who were their sons or husbands. In the Nineteenth Dynasty, for example, Ramesses II

Nefertiri, tomb of Nefertiri, Thebes

(1304–1238 BC), who is reminiscent of Amenhotep III in that he accepted foreign princesses as his minor wives, and married two of his daughters, built for his favourite wife, Nefertiri, a magnificent tomb at Thebes, and a mortuary temple next to his own at Abu Simbel in Nubia. Whether he did so purely out of devotion to her, or simply as an excuse to build yet more monuments, we cannot know. Neither can we know, for lack of evidence, how much power these royal favourites exercised over their sons and husbands; however, it seems safe to assume from comparisons with later, better documented, eras that they sometimes interfered in matters of state.

Nefertiri and Isis, tomb of Nefertiri, Thebes

Many of the minor wives of the Kings of Egypt must have led frustrated lives. Their only hope of exerting influence lay with having a son who might become crown prince and, in due course, king. In theory, any son of the king, or, indeed, any man, could lay claim to the throne by marrying the royal heiress. If, therefore, the 'Great Royal Wife' had no son, her daughter, the royal heiress, would be married to a son of one of the king's other wives, that is, to her half-brother. The mother of Hatshepsut (see page 140), for example, had no son; Hatshepsut was married, therefore, to the son of a minor wife of her father. Hatshepsut herself had a daughter, Neferure, but no son, and so her husband's son by a minor wife was made crown prince through marriage to Neferure, the royal heiress.

In the Twentieth Dynasty a minor wife of Ramesses III (1198–1166 BC), the last great King of Egypt, plotted to kill him so that her son might inherit the throne. She persuaded several of her husband's concubines and some of the royal servants to help her. At first, they tried to murder Ramesses by magical means, using wax dolls; when these proved ineffectual, they sent messages to their relatives outside the palace asking them to raise a rebellion. The rebellion failed, and the conspirators were brought to trial. According to the records of the trial, those found guilty were allowed to die 'by their own hand'. The fates of the prince who would be king and of his mother are not recorded.

After the fall of the Twentieth Dynasty, Egypt began a long period of decline, embarking upon what is now called the Third Intermediate Period (Twenty-first to Twenty-fourth Dynasties, 1085–715 BC), followed by the Late Period (Twenty-fifth to Thirtieth Dynasties, 716–332 BC). The last king of the Twentieth Dynasty, Ramesses XI (1113–1085 BC), was powerless to prevent the Theban region being made into a principality independent of the kings in the north, who ruled the rest of Egypt from Tanis in the Delta.

The move to independence was initiated in Thebes by an army general named Herihor, who became First Prophet (High Priest) of Amun, controller of the vast possessions of the state god of Egypt. Herihor's successors became military pontiffs, exercising sovereign power over Thebes, with three of them writing their names in cartouches after the fashion of the kings of Egypt. These priestly kings of Thebes ruled over both the living and the dead. They wielded their power over the living by announcing not only religious but also administrative and judicial decisions by means of the Oracle of Amun, and persuading the populace to accept their policies as the will of the god. They were also responsible for the Theban necropolis, part of which housed the tombs of the kings of Egypt of the three New Kingdom dynasties.

Relations between Thebes and Tanis were friendly enough. The Tanite kings of the Twenty-first Dynasty (1085–945 BC) accepted the independence of the priestly kings, and cemented the friendship by using princesses of the royal house as instruments of policy. The method employed was marriage, princesses being sent from Tanis to Thebes to marry High Priests of Amun. The advantage of this to the king in Tanis is clear enough, in that he had placed his daughter in a position in which she could exert considerable influence on his behalf. The high priests possibly considered that the presence in Thebes of a princess of the royal house conferred legitimacy upon them. Thus, the High Priest Piankh (1090–1082 BC) married Princess Henttowy of Tanis, and their son, Pinudjem I (1082–1052 BC), married two Tanite princesses – first, Makare, and then her niece, Esemkhebe. From Pinudjem's time onwards the High Priests of Amun were descended through the female line from Tanite kings. Henttowy and Makare were made much of by Pinudjem, appearing with him in many reliefs.

An interesting sidelight on the relationship between a High Priest of Amun and his wife is provided by a papyrus found at Deir el-Bahri.[15] In it, reference is made to Neskhons, the wife of Pinudjem II (987–969 BC):

> I will turn the heart of Neskhons, the daughter of Thendhout, and she shall not do any evil thing to Pinudjem, the child of Isimkheb [sic]; I will turn her heart, and will not allow her to curtail his life; I will turn her heart, and will not allow her to cause to be done to him anything which is detrimental to the heart of a living man.

On her marriage Makare was given the titles 'Divine Wife of Amun' and 'Divine Votaress'. The title, 'Divine Wife of Amun', came into being in the Eighteenth Dynasty, but was not at first used to refer to the high priestess at Thebes. It was originally that of a king's daughter who was destined to become queen and who could bear it as a child, when she was usually betrothed to the heir apparent. The title was thus one that belonged to the royal heiress. If the royal heiress died before her father, then both title and heir apparent were transferred to another daughter of the king. If the heir apparent died before the reigning king, then the 'Divine Wife of Amun' was betrothed or married to another son. Clearly, the

'Divine Wife' did not obtain her title because she was queen, but became queen by virtue of being 'Divine Wife'.

The title descended from mother to daughter, and both could bear it simultaneously, as did Hatshepsut and her daughter, Neferure. The weakness of the system lay in the impossibility of ensuring that every 'Divine Wife' bore a daughter. In any case, it was abandoned during the Amarna Period, when Tiy (see page 151) and Nefertiti (see page 151) became queens although they were not of royal blood. The title was revived in the Nineteenth Dynasty, but with a difference. The wives of Ramesses I and Seti I were each called 'Divine Wife of Amun', but they were not daughters of kings. None of the wives of Ramesses II bore the title, possibly because Ramesses came from a Delta family and the title was special to Thebes. The only other 'Divine Wife of Amun' in the Nineteenth Dynasty was Tausert, the wife of King Siptah, who may have been the daughter of Seti II. Thus, in the Nineteenth Dynasty, 'Divine wife of Amun' had become little more than a title of the queen.[16]

In Makare's time the title 'Divine Wife of Amun' meant that the wife of the High Priest of Amun at Thebes was considered, for religious purposes, to be the embodiment on earth of the god's wife. Obviously, this had not precluded her from marrying and having children by her mortal husband. In the Twenty-third Dynasty, however, a new development in the significance of the title took place. The fourth king of that dynasty, Osorkon III (777–749 BC), made a determined effort to assert more control over Thebes. Osorkon, evidently a forceful king, somehow managed to prevail upon the reigning High Priest of Amun to accept the transfer of the estates and property of Amun to the 'Divine Wife of Amun', thereby diminishing his own power. For the next two hundred years or so the position of each High Priest of Amun at Thebes was that of a mere religious figure-head, the power formerly wielded by holders of that office being exercised by the holder of the office of 'Divine Wife of Amun'.

From Osorkon III's time onwards, the title 'Divine Wife of Amun' was that of a daughter of the king who became the consecrated wife of the god, Amun. She was expected to reside in Thebes and to remain celibate throughout her life. Each 'Divine Wife' had a second title, that of 'Hand of the God', possibly a reference to one of the creation legends in which the god, Atum, was said to have brought his children into existence by means of masturbation. She was equipped with attendants who were considered to be the concubines of Amun and who, like herself, were expected to be celibate. Being officially celibate and without children of her own, each 'Divine Wife of Amun'[17] had to ensure the succession by adopting a 'daughter', who was recognized as the heiress presumptive, and who, it has been suggested, bore the title 'Divine Votaress'. The reigning king took pains to ensure that it was one of his daughters who became the 'Divine Votaress'.

The 'Divine Wives of Amun' owned great estates by virtue of their position and employed a large number of officials to administer them. Because of their enormous wealth, which enabled them to wield temporal power, and because of their religious position, through which they wielded spiritual power, they also enjoyed a considerable amount of political influence. The authority of a 'Divine Wife of Amun' was limited only by the fact that it was not exercised outside the Theban area. In Thebes, at least, she was regarded as the equal of her royal father and was depicted in temple reliefs making the offerings to the gods – elsewhere, it was always the king who was shown carrying out these rituals (but see page 154).

Upon her succession a 'Divine Wife' was accorded a formal investiture and a coronation. Since she was the symbolic monarch of Thebes, she was addressed as 'Your Majesty', although she never bore the title of queen; and given a Throne Name, an element of which was often 'Mut', the name of the goddess who was Amun's wife. In inscriptions the name of the 'Divine Wife' was written inside a cartouche as though she were a ruling monarch. Her death was described officially in the same way as that of a king (see page 170); she was accorded a royal burial and a mortuary temple in which offerings were made to her 'throughout eternity'. The most famous of these mortuary temples (see page 170) were built between the eighth and sixth centuries BC in the precincts of the great temple of Medinet Habu, the mortuary temple of Ramesses III (1198–1166 BC).

It is difficult to establish what the duties of the 'Divine Wife of Amun' were. The stelae recording the adoptions of two of the 'Wives',

Temple of Divine Votaresses, Medinet Habu

Nitocris and Ankhnesneferibre (see pages 168, 170), make it clear that they had considerable properties and revenues at their disposal. Presumably it was expected of the 'Divine Wives' that they use a good part of their wealth to ensure that Theban officials remained loyal not only to them but also to the reigning king. In all probability, the chief duty of the 'Divine Wife' would have been to make known the will of Amun through oracular means, just as the high priests before them had done. It is not difficult to appreciate that the manipulation of the Oracle of Amun, enabling the 'Divine Wife' to maintain control over the devotees of Amun who held important posts in the Thebaid, made her a valuable agent of her father.

Ramesses III and his ladies, Medinet Habu (see page 157)

From the reign of Osorkon III (777–749 BC) to that of Psam-metichus III (526–525 BC), Thebes was ruled by a succession of five daughters of the ruling royal house. The first of these was Shepen-wepet I, who, sometime around 754 BC, was appointed 'Divine Wife of Amun' by her father, Osorkon III. She was given the full cartouches of a king, and officiated at the temple of Osiris, Ruler of Eternity. Shepenwepet I continued in power under Osorkon III's successor, Takeloth III (754–734 BC). During his reign, there is no mention of the 'Divine Wife of Amun' in the records, and he does not seem to have made arrangements for a daughter of his own to be adopted by Shepenwepet I. In 740 BC, Piankhi, the ruler of Kush (modern Sudan), which had once been part of the Egyptian empire and where Amun was worshipped with devotion, invaded Thebes and installed his sister, Amenirdis I,[18] as 'Divine Wife Apparent'. When Shepenwepet I died, she was buried, along with several members of her family, in a vault beneath the floor of her mortuary chapel at Medinet Habu.[19]

Piankhi went on to conquer the whole of Egypt, becoming the

Shepenwepet I, High Priestess of Amun, Medinet Habu

first ruler of the Twenty-fifth Dynasty (748–654 BC). In 710 BC, Amenirdis I adopted her niece, Shepenwepet II, Piankhi's daughter; and some years later, Shepenwepet II adopted Amenirdis II, the daughter of Taharqa (690–664 BC). When Amenirdis I died, it was her niece, Shepenwepet II, the new 'Divine Wife', who completed a mortuary chapel at Medinet Habu for her. Nothing now remains in the burial vault beneath this chapel, but many of

Amenirdis I

Amenirdis I's grave goods are to be found in museums all over the world, while a fine alabaster statue of her standing on a base of black granite is in Cairo Museum.

On the lintel above the doorway of Amenirdis I's chapel, an 'Appeal to the Living' is inscribed in which passers-by are enjoined to pray for the deceased:

O ye living who are upon earth and pass by this Ka House which Shepenwepet made . . . for Amenirdis, deceased: as you love your children, and would bequeath to them your positions, your houses, your lakes and your canals . . . and as your wives perform rites for Hathor, Lady of the West, who causes them to bear males and females to you without illness or suffering, and without your suffering for them, or experiencing suffering or affliction – Please [pray].

For most of Taharqa's reign, Egypt seems to have been fairly united and prosperous. But in 671 BC, he was challenged on Egyptian soil by the King of Assyria, Esarhaddon. Taharqa fled to Kush, leaving behind his wives and children for Esarhaddon to capture, and the Assyrians took over the Delta, confirming a local prince, Necho of Sais, as its ruler. In 664 BC, Taharqa died. His successor, Tantamani, had a dream promising him Egypt and so marched north to claim it. He killed Necho of Sais, whose son, Psammetichus, fled to Assyria. Assurbanipal, King of Assyria, marched on Egypt, driving Tantamani back south. In 663 BC, the Assyrians sacked Thebes. The dreadful event is described in the Bible thus:

Populous No [No Amon, the City of Amun, i.e. Thebes] . . . Ethiopia [by which is meant Kush] and Egypt were her strength, and it was infinite . . . Yet was she carried away, she went into captivity: her young children also were dashed in pieces at the top of all the streets: and they cast lots for her honourable men, and all her great men were bound in chains.[20]

In spite of all this, the 'Divine Wife' Shepenwepet II remained in place!

For a time the Delta was ruled by petty princes acting as Assyrian vassals. Strongest of them was Psammetichus, who, as an Assyrian puppet, became the supreme prince in the region, the first ruler of the Twenty-sixth Dynasty (672–525 BC). In Middle Egypt a dynasty of shipmasters ruled in Herakleopolis, whence they had control over all the river traffic that sailed upstream; and gradually, Psammetichus formed an alliance with them in which they recognized his overlordship. Thebes, meanwhile, still considered that its rulers were the Kushites.

For the first few years of his reign, Psammetichus I was careful to keep his status of Assyrian vassal, thus avoiding the risk of Assyrian intervention. But eight years after he came to the throne, Psammetichus opened negotiations with Thebes. By the next year, 656 BC, Egypt was united and a short time later, Psammetichus was able to declare independence from Assyria, which by that time was having problems holding its empire together. The alliance with Thebes, which was obviously essential to Psammetichus's plans for an independent Egypt, was cemented by the appointment of Psammetichus's daughter, Nitocris, as 'Divine Wife of Amun Apparent'.

At that time political power in Thebes lay not with the 'Divine Wife of Amun', nor with the High Priest of Amun, but with a man who held a minor priestly office – Montuemhet, who was only Fourth Prophet of Amun but mayor of the city and governor of Upper Egypt. The Twenty-fifth Dynasty king, Taharqa, had installed Montuemhet in Thebes while he himself resided at Tanis in the Delta. When Taharqa was driven out of Egypt by Esarhaddon in 671 BC, the victorious Assyrian confirmed Montuemhet in office as his vassal. In his inscriptions,[21] Montuemhet boasts of 'protecting the city' of Thebes, presumably by changing his allegiance from Taharqa to Esarhaddon; and of making extensive repairs to the city and conducting ceremonies of purification in the despoiled temples.

When Psammetichus became king, recognized by the Assyrians as their vassal overlord of the whole of Egypt, Montuemhet found it politic to negotiate with him. Montuemhet's position does not seem to have been strong, and in a treaty of 659 or 658 BC, he agreed to accept Psammetichus's daughter as 'Divine Wife of Amun' and to allow Psammetichus to appoint not only her officials but also the governor and border commander of the area to the south of Thebes. In return, Montuemhet was allowed to retain his position as mayor of Thebes, but only for the duration of his lifetime – any claim by his son to inherit it was not recognized. However, his status was emphasized by his magnificent tomb near Deir el-Bahri,[22] which has a vast underground complex and an enormous sun-court adorned with statues of Montuemhet. The large mud-brick pylon which marks the entrance to the tomb still dominates the Plain of Asasif.

Psammetichus seemingly had little difficulty in persuading Montuemhet to accept Princess Nitocris as 'Divine Wife Apparent' – the position had, after all, been an instrument of royal policy for the last hundred years, and Montuemhet would have expected the reigning king to install his own daughter as his surrogate in Thebes. But what part, if any, the reigning 'Divine Wife', Shepenwepet II, played in the adoption of Nitocris is not known. She already had an adopted daughter, Amenirdis II; and it seems that these two ladies were unswervingly loyal to the Nubian, Tantamani, as an inscription in Thebes dated to 657 BC reveals.[23] Possibly Shepenwepet II prevaricated, for Nitocris did not arrive in Thebes until 655 BC – some months after the death of Tantamani.

Nitocris's adoption as 'Divine Wife of Amun' was recorded on a great granite stele which was erected in the temple of Amun at Karnak, but which is now in Cairo Museum.[24] It describes how, in the spring of 655 BC, Nitocris and a large retinue boarded ships – the stele does not state where but presumably it was either in Memphis or, more probably, in her father's capital city, Sais. The great fleet, fittingly under the command of the shipmaster, Semtutefnakhte, governor of the Herakleopolitan nome, sailed to Thebes (a journey which took sixteen days), where, in a grand ceremony, Nitocris was formally adopted.

Because the 'mother' of the adopted 'daughter' is not named in the stele, but only referred to as 'she' or 'her', it has been suggested that Nitocris was adopted not by Shepenwepet II, the reigning 'Divine Wife', but by the 'Divine Wife Apparent', Amenirdis II, on the grounds that Psammetichus, eager to be seen to act uprightly, would not have wanted to displace Amenirdis II. It is difficult to envisage, however, that Psammetichus would have been prepared for his daughter to occupy a secondary position to Amenirdis II for an indefinite number of years – she would thereby have had to wait for the deaths of two women, one of whom must have been relatively young, before being in the position of greatest use to her father, the king. It is more likely that Nitocris was adopted at once by Shepenwepet II as her heiress and successor and that

Amenirdis II, rather than stay in Thebes stripped of her former high position, returned to Kush with her major-domo, Akhamenron, and other officials.[25] She is not buried at Medinet Habu like the other 'Divine Wives', so presumably her tomb is in Kush.

Whether or not Nitocris became 'Divine Wife Apparent', only second in line to Amenirdis II, she was endowed with the lands and revenues of Amun immediately upon her arrival in Thebes. She was also given estates 'both up the river and down' by her father – 1,800 *arouras* of land in seven nomes of Upper Egypt and 1,400 in four nomes in the Delta, equivalent to some 2,000 acres in all. Psammetichus claimed that he had 'endowed her better than those who had gone before her', not an idle boast judging from the lists of property on the stele.[26] It was probably with revenues from these estates that she rewarded her officials – many of whom came to Thebes with her from the Delta and thus had no ties with Thebes – thereby ensuring their loyalty not only to herself but also to the father who was the ultimate source of their rewards.

The officials of a 'Divine Wife of Amun' must sometimes have been troubled by conflicting loyalties. The king was all powerful in Egypt as a whole, but the lady herself held sway in Thebes, and it was in Thebes that they were serving. The tussle between a 'Divine Wife' and the king over her personnel was probably most acute in the years just after her accession. The death of a 'Divine Wife of Amun' did not necessarily involve an immediate change in the top personnel of her palace. Instead, the new 'Divine Wife' left them in place while she found her feet and then perhaps replaced them with her own favourites, or as many of them as she could, given that the king would try to put his own men in place.

The 'Divine Wife of Amun' did not administer her vast wealth herself; this task fell to her chief steward or major-domo. In her sixty-nine years in Thebes (655–586 BC), Nitocris had at least four. The first was Pabasa, whose tomb[27] on the plain in front of Deir el-Bahri is marked like Montuemhet's by a large mud-brick pylon. Pabasa was succeeded in about 638 BC by Ibe. The fathers of these two men each held the title 'Beloved of the God', which is thought to be one conferred upon them by the king, he being the god referred to in the title.[28] Hence, Pabasa and Ibe were the sons of men who did not come from Thebes but from Sais, where they were favourite courtiers of the king. It seems that Psammetichus pro-moted the sons of his courtiers to the post of major-domo to the 'Divine Wife of Amun' confident that they would place loyalty to him above the interests of Thebes and its high priestess.

A report dated to the twenty-sixth year of Psammetichus's reign (638 BC) makes it clear that although Ibe was responsible to Nitocris for the management of her estates, when it came to large-scale building works it was the king to whom he had to apply for permission, for the materials needed were under the control of the monarch. Ibe recorded that

His Majesty sent those who were in his suite . . . of the South-land, prophets and priests of Amun and sacred women of Amun. They came saying 'His Majesty has heard that the house of the Divine Wife of Amun is beginning to fall into ruin.'[29]

Ibe was instructed to effect repairs and assured that he had been given the authority to do so, and would receive any materials necessary.

Ibe died in the same year, 610 BC, as Psammetichus. The next three kings, Necho II, Psammetichus II and Apries, were unable to prevent Nitocris exerting her independence and appointing her own men, first Padihorresnet, followed in due course by Sheshonq, as her major-domos. Padihorresnet was the son of the chief scribe and chamberlain of the 'Divine Wife' and Sheshonq was the son of Harsiese, the overseer of her chamberlains. Thus, Nitocris's last two major-domos were not men of Sais but of Thebes, and owed their loyalty to her rather than to the king in Sais.

For over fifty years, the 'Divine Wife of Amun', Nitocris, man-aged to avoid adopting a successor. By so doing, she made sure that the kings of Egypt were unable to send their own men into Thebes as part of the retinue of the 'Divine Wife Apparent'. But in 594 BC, the aged Nitocris, who must have been in her eighties, adopted her great niece, Ankhnesneferibre, the daughter of Psammetichus II. Ankhnesneferibre arrived in Thebes within a year of her father coming to the throne; and, in addition to being adopted by Nitocris, was invested as First Prophet (High Priest) of Amun, a position not accorded to any other 'Divine Wife'.[30]

Eight years after adopting Ankhnesneferibre, on 16 December 586 BC, Nitocris died. Her death was recorded on a stele now in the Cairo Museum,[31] using the same phrases as those used to mark the passing of a King of Egypt:

> Year 4 of Apries, 4th month of Shomu, day 4, the Divine Wife Nitocris, justified, was raised up to heaven, being united with the sun's disk, the divine flesh being merged with him who made it.

Nitocris was buried at Medinet Habu. Just as Shepenwepet II had completed a mortuary chapel for her predecessor (see page 163), so Nitocris had completed the mortuary chapel at Medinet Habu which was left unfinished at Shepenwepet II's death. Nitocris then added a burial chamber for herself alongside that belonging to Shepenwepet II; and later added another for her real mother, Queen Mehytenweskhet. The three burials were pillaged in antiquity, but Nitocris's sarcophagus was found in a shaft at Deir el-Medina and is now in the Cairo Museum.

Twelve days after the death of Nitocris, on the sixteenth day of the fourth month of Shomu, Ankhnesneferibre was invested with the office of 'Divine Wife of Amun'. It seems that the new 'Divine Wife' was not as formidable as her late aunt, Nitocris. She inherited Nitocris's major-domo, Sheshonq, son of Harsiese, but when Sheshonq died, she was powerless to prevent the reigning king, Amasis (570–526 BC), from foisting on her as major-domo first his own man, Padineith, the son of one of his courtiers, and in due course, Padineith's son, Sheshonq. When Cambyses, King of Persia, conquered Egypt in 525 BC, Ankhnesneferibre was an old lady who had been the 'Divine Wife of Amun' for over sixty years. How long she survived after the Persian conquest is not known, but the office of 'Divine Wife of Amun' died with her, and Thebes, like the rest of Egypt, became part of the Persian Empire.

Ankhnesneferibre is thought to have been buried at Medinet Habu in a fourth chapel there, now vanished. Her sarcophagus, like that of Nitocris, was found at Deir el-Medina, having been re-used by a man who died during the reign of the Emperor Augustus. Now one of the finest pieces in the Egyptian Sculpture Gallery in the British Museum,[32] it is a rectangular stone chest inscribed with texts from the *Book of the Dead*.[33] On the bottom of the interior of the sarcophagus is a low-relief representation of the goddess, Hathor; and on the outside of its lid, Ankhnesneferibre herself is sculpted. She is depicted as a lady whose nose is rather more fleshy than the delicate noses so often portrayed in standard Egyptian relief, wearing a long pleated dress with shawl sleeves. On her head she wears the vulture skullcap, the two feathers and the sun's disc set between two horns, as worn by queens. In her hands she carries the crook and the flail, symbols of royal authority. The lid is decorated on the underside with a carved figure of the sky goddess, Nut, stretching out over the body in the sarcophagus in eternal protection, a task she failed to accomplish since the body of the 'Divine Wife' has vanished.

Ankhnesneferibre was adopted by Nitocris, who was then in her seventies, in 595 BC. She assumed office in 586 BC and was still alive some sixty years later. Thus, two of the formidable ladies who held the office of 'Divine Wife of Amun' between them reigned for over 130 years. The temperament of the divine ladies is hinted at in the lines which follow the 'polite request' to passers-by to pray for the 'Divine Wife' that is carved on the lintel of Amenirdis I's chapel at Medinet Habu:

> As for those who do not recite the prayers – may the Mistress of the West cause them to be sick and their wives to be afflicted!

Although the 'Divine Wives of Amun' held extraordinary power, it was restricted to the Theban area, and was held at some cost to themselves in that they were denied the right to a 'normal' life with husband and children, a right denied them by the laws imposed by men of power. As for 'women of power' – it is perhaps instructive that, Ptolemaic queens apart, in three thousand years of Egyptian history only four women held the highest position in the land, that of queen regnant. Otherwise royal women exerted influence only through or upon their husbands and sons. Considering that in

ancient Egypt women as a whole were never regarded as a part of
society to be oppressed, it is perhaps surprising that there were not
more women of power and political influence in all sections of
society.

REFERENCES

Abbreviations

Ostraca and papyri: according to convention, *P.* is used for papyrus and O. for ostracon, followed by an identification, usually the site where discovered, e.g. *P. Oxyrhynchus*, or the present location of the ostracon, e.g. O. Strassburg.

Ann. Serv.	*Annales du Service des Antiquités de l'Égypte.*
ARE	J.H. Breasted, *Ancient Records of Egypt*, Chicago, 1906.
BIÉ	*Bulletin de l'Institut Égyptologique.*
CAH	*Cambridge Ancient History*, Cambridge University Press.
Cd'É	*Chronique d'Égypte.*
JEA	*Journal of Egyptian Archaeology.*
ZÄS	*Zeitschrift für Ägyptische Sprache und Altertumskunde.*

Notes to Introduction

1. W.M.F. Petrie, *Social life in ancient Egypt*, London, 1924, pp. v-vi.
2. W.S. Blackman, 'Some social and religious customs in modern Egypt', *Bulletin de la Société Géographie d'Égypte*, XIV, 1926, p. 48.

Bibliography to Introduction

ANDERSON, A.S., 'Mirrors of the past', *Aramco World Magazine*, 34(4), 1983, pp. 24–32.

ANDREWS, C., *Egyptian mummies*, London, 1984.

BLACKMAN, W.S., *The* fellahin *of Upper Egypt*, London, 1927.

BOWMAN, A.K., *Egypt after the pharaohs*, London, 1986.

COCKBURN, A. & E., *Mummies, diseases and ancient cultures*, Cambridge, 1983.

——, *The Egyptian mummy: secrets and science*, University Museum Handbook, No. 1, Philadelphia, 1980.

DAVID, A.R., *Evidence embalmed*, Manchester, 1984.

DAVIES, N. de G., *The mastaba of Ptahhetep and Akhethetep*, vols I–II, London, 1900–01.

DAWSON, W.R. and GRAY, P.H.K., *Catalogue of Egyptian antiquities in the British Museum I: Mummies and human remains*, London, 1968.

DIODORUS SICULUS, *Library of History* (translated by C.H. Oldfather *et al.*), Loeb Classical Library, Cambridge, Mass., and London.

DUELL, P., *The mastaba of Mereruka*, vols I–II, Chicago, 1938.

EPRON, L., DAUMAS, F. and WILD, H., *Le tombeau de Ti*, vols I–III, Cairo, 1939–66.

GRAY, P.H.K. and SLOW, D., 'Egyptian mummies in the City of Liverpool Museums': *Liverpool Bulletin Museums Number*, vol. 15, 1968.

HAMILTON-PATERSON, J. and ANDREWS, C., *Mummies: Death and life in ancient Egypt*, London, 1978.

HARRIS, J.E. and WEEKS, K.R., *X-raying the pharaohs*, London, 1973.

HARRIS, J.E. and WENTE, E.F.(eds), *An X-ray atlas of the royal mummies*, Chicago, 1980.

HERODOTUS, *The Histories* (translated by A. de Selincourt), Penguin Classics, Harmondsworth, 1972.

LANE, E., *The manners and customs of the modern Egyptians*, Everyman Edition, London, 1966.

LEWIS, N., *Life in Egypt under Roman rule*, Oxford, 1983.

LLOYD, A.B., *Herodotus Book II*, Introduction, Leiden, 1975.

——, *Herodotus Book II*, Commentary 1–98, Leiden, 1976.

MACFARQUHAR, C.F., *Early Greek travellers in Egypt, Greece and Rome*, 13, 1966, pp. 108–16.

MANNICHE, L., *City of the dead: Thebes in Egypt*, London, 1987.

PAABO, S., 'Molecular cloning of ancient Egyptian mummy DNA', *Nature*, vol. 314, 18 April 1985, pp. 644–5.

SPENCER, A.J., *Death in ancient Egypt*, Harmondsworth, 1982.
STRABO, *The Geography* (translated by H.L. Jones), Loeb
  Classical Library, Cambridge, Mass., and London.

Notes to Chapter One

1. J.A. Omlin, *Der Papyrus 55001 und seine satirisch-erotischen Zeichnungen und Inschriften*, Turin, 1973; and L. Manniche, *Sexual life in ancient Egypt*, London, 1987, pp. 106–15.
2. Love poems: the poems quoted in this book are the author's own translations; variant translations and further examples of poems can be found in M. Lichtheim, *Ancient Egyptian Literature*, vol. II, Berkeley and Los Angeles, 1976, pp. 182–93.
3. For the Instruction of Ankhsheshonq see Lichtheim, *op. cit.*, vol. III, 1980, pp. 159–84.
4. For the Instruction of the Insinger Papyrus see Lichtheim, *op. cit.*, vol. III, pp. 184–217.
5. For translations of the Westcar Papyrus see Lichtheim, *op. cit.*, vol. I, 1973, pp. 215–22; and A. Erman, *The ancient Egyptians: a sourcebook of their writings*, New York, 1966, pp. 36–47.
6. For the Story of the Two Brothers see Lichtheim, *op. cit.*, vol. II, pp. 203–11; and Erman, *op. cit.*, pp. 150–61.
7. For the story of Khamwese and Tabubu see Lichtheim, *op. cit.*, vol. III, pp. 127–38.
8. For the Doomed Prince see Lichtheim, *op. cit.*, vol. II, pp. 200–3; and Erman, *op.cit.*, pp. 161–5.
9. Apuleius, *The golden ass*, Harmondsworth, 1950, p. 271.

Bibliography to Chapter One

Art

ALDRED, C., *Old Kingdom art in ancient Egypt*, London, 1949.
——, *Middle Kingdom art in ancient Egypt 2300–1590 BC*, London, 1950.

——, *New Kingdom art in ancient Egypt during the Eighteenth Dynasty 1570–1320 BC*, 2nd edition, London, 1961.

——, *Egyptian art*, London, 1980.

IVERSEN, E., *Canon and proportion in Egyptian art*, 2nd ed., Warminster, 1975.

MEKHITARIAN, A., *Egyptian painting* (translated by S. Gilbert), Geneva, 1954, rp, 1978.

MICHALOWSKI, K., *The art of ancient Egypt*, London, 1969.

ROBINS, G., *Egyptian painting and relief*, Aylesbury, 1986.

SCHAFER, H., *Principles of Egyptian art* (translated by J. Baines), Oxford, 1974.

SMITH, W.S., *A history of Egyptian sculpture and painting in the Old Kingdom*, 2nd edition, Oxford, 1949.

——, *The art and architecture of ancient Egypt*, 2nd ed, Harmondsworth, 1981.

VANDIER, J. and NAGUIB, M., *Egypt, paintings from tombs and temples*, New York, 1954.

WILKINSON, C.K. and HILL, M., *Egyptian wall paintings: the Metropolitan Museum of Art's collection of facsimiles*, New York, 1983.

WOLDERING, I., *Egypt: the art of the pharaohs* (translated by A. Keep), Baden-Baden, 1963.

Erotic symbolism

DERCHAIN, P., *La perruque et le cristal, Studien zur altägyptischen Kultur*, 2, 1975, pp. 55–74.

——, 'Le lotus, le mandragore et le perséa', *Cd'É*, 50, 1975, pp. 65–86.

MANNICHE, L., *Sexual life in ancient Egypt*, London, 1987.

——, 'Some aspects of ancient Egyptian sexual life', *Acta Orientalia*, 38, 1977, pp. 11–23.

Death and religion

HART, G., *A dictionary of Egyptian gods and goddesses*, London, 1984.

HEYROB, S.K., 'The cult of Isis among women in the

Graeco-Roman world': *Études préliminaires aux religions orientales dans l'empire romain*, vol. 51, Leiden, 1975.

LURKER, M., *The gods and symbols of ancient Egypt* (translated by P. Clayton), London, 1974.

MORENZ, S., *Egyptian religion* (translated by A. Keep), London, 1973.

SAUNERON, S., *Les prêtres de l'ancienne Égypte*, Paris, 1957.

SPENCER, A.J., *Death in ancient Egypt*, Harmondsworth, 1982.

WARNER, M., *Alone of all her sex*, London, 1985.

WATTERSON, B., *The gods of ancient Egypt*, London, 1984.

Notes to Chapter Two

1. The term *'nh n niwt*, lit: 'who lives in the city' is translated conventionally as 'citizeness', but its exact meaning is obscure. Pestman suggests that a woman who is described thus is either married or a widow (P.W. Pestman, *Marriage and matrimonial property in ancient Egypt*, Leiden, 1961, p. 11, note 2).

2. B.G. Trigger, *et al.*, *Ancient Egypt: a social history*, Cambridge, 1983, p. 192.

3. World survey – Women in agriculture – presented to the World Conference to review and appraise the achievements of the United Nations decade for women: *Equality, development and peace*, Nairobi, 1985, p. 16.

4. Herodotus, *The Histories*, II, 35, Penguin Classics, 1965.

5. S.B. Pomeroy, *Women in hellenistic Egypt*, New York, 1984, p. 172.

6. *P. Oxyrhynchus*, 1380, ll.214–16.

7. e.g. J. Pirenne, 'Le statut de la femme dans l'ancienne Égypte': *Recueil Jean Bodin XI*, p. 63 foll.; others cited by Pestman, *op. cit.*, p. 182, note 3.

8. H. Thompson, *A family archive from Siut*, Oxford, 1934, Text, p. xvi.

9. *P. Grenfell*, I, xxvii.

10. *ibid.* xxxiii.

11. *P. Brooklyn*, 16.205; R.A. Parker, *A Saite oracle papyrus from Thebes*, Providence, 1962, p. 50.

12. Pomeroy, *op. cit.*, p. 103 foll.

13. Pomeroy, *op. cit.*, p. 111.

14. Two and a half *artaba* is about 75 kilograms; the average monthly ration of wheat for a man was 1 *artab* (C. Préaux, *Le monde hellénistique*, 2 vols, Paris, 1978, p. 364).

15. *P. Grenfell*, xxi.

16. *ibid.*

17. *P. Giessen*, II, 36; demotic version of same text, *P. Strassburg demotic*, WG 16.

18. *P. Heidleberg*, 1280 + *P. Grenfell*, I, xv & xvii.

19. *P. London*, II, 401, p. 13.

20. *P. Giessen*, II, 37.

21. *P. Heidleberg demotic*, 739 a.

22. *P. Grenfell*, I, xix.

23. *ibid.*, xx.

24. *ibid.*, xvii.

25. M.S. Tichener, *Guardianship of women in Egypt during the Ptolemaic and Roman eras: University of Wisconsin Studies in Language and Literature*, vol. 15, Madison, 1922, pp. 20–8.

26. *P. Grenfell*, I, xviii.

27. *ibid.*, xix.

28. *ibid.*, xx.

29. W.C. Hayes, *A papyrus of the late Middle Kingdom in the Brooklyn Museum*, Brooklyn, 1955, p. 114 foll.

30. *P. Louvre*, 2443.

31. For example, *P. Louvre*, 3231a, in which an unmarried woman of the Twenty-seventh Dynasty named Ruru purchased land; also *P. Philadelphia*, 26 (212 BC).

32. For example, wages for weaving cloth – *P. Louvre*, 3168; wages for arranging a funeral – *P. Louvre*, 3228 (both Twenty-fifth Dynasty); also a New Kingdom example in Ostraca of the Institut Français d'Archéologie Orientale, 539.

33. For example, O. Deir el-Medina, 112; O. Colin Campbell, 23 (both Twentieth Dynasty).

34. *P. Bulaq*, x, 8; *P. Rylands*, II; *P. Louvre*, 2439, 2429b; *P. Philadelphia*, 13.

35. Trigger, *op. cit.*, pp. 314–15.

36. A.H. Gardiner, 'A Dynasty XX deed of adoption': *JEA*, 26, 1960, p. 23 foll.; E. Cruz-Uribe, 'A new look at the Adoption Papyrus': *JEA*, 74, 1988, pp. 220–3.

37. J. Černy, 'The will of Naunakhte': *JEA*, 31, 1945, p. 29 foll.

38. A.H. Gardiner, 'The inscriptions of Mes': *Untersuchungen zur Geschichte und Alterumskunde Ägyptens*, ed. K. Sethe, vol. IV, Leipzig, 1905.

Bibliography to Chapter Two

ČERNY, J., *Catalogue des ostraca hiératiques non littéraires de Deir el Medineh*, Documents de Fouilles, Cairo, 1935 seq. Continued by S. Sauneron.

PIRENNE, J., 'Le statut de la femme dans l'ancienne Égypte': *Recueil de la Société Jean Bodin XI*, 'La Femme', Brussels, 1959, pp. 63–77.

POMEROY, S.B., 'Apollonia (also called Senmonthis), wife of Dryton: woman of two cultures': paper delivered at the colloquium on 'Social history and the papyri', Columbia University, 9 April 1983.

——, 'The married woman: honour and shame in Ptolemaic Egypt': paper presented before the Society for the Study of Egyptian Antiquities at the University of Toronto, 22 November 1980.

——, *Women in Hellenistic Egypt: From Alexander to Cleopatra*, New York, 1984.

PRÉAUX, C., 'Le statut de la femme à l'époque Hellénistique, principalement en Égypte': *Recueil Jean Bodin XI*, pp. 127–75.

REVILLOUT, E., *Précis du droit Égyptien*, Paris, 1903.

TAUBENSCHLAG, R., 'La compétence du *kyrios* dans le droit Graeco-Romain': *Archives d'Histoire de Droit Oriental*, 2. 1938, p. 293 foll.

——, *The law of Graeco-Roman Egypt in the light of the papyri*, 2nd ed., Warsaw, 1955.

THEODORIDES, A., 'Le droit matrimonial dans l'Égypte pharaonique': *Revue Internationale des Droits de l'Antiquité*, 3e série, 23, 1976, pp. 15–55.

——, 'Le problème du droit égyptien ancien': Le Droit égyptien ancien – Colloque organisé par l'Institut des Hautes Études Belgique, 18–19 Mars 1974, Brussels, p. 3 foll.

Notes to Chapter Three

1. A.J. Spencer, *Death in ancient Egypt*, Harmondsworth, 1982, pp. 67–8.

2. E. Boserup, *Women's role in economic development*, New York, 1970.

3. F.Ll. Griffith, *Hieratic papyri from Kahun and Gurob*, vol. II, London, 1898, vii, 1.

4. B. Lesko, *The remarkable women of ancient Egypt*, Providence, 1987, p. 20.

5. H.G. Fischer, *Egyptian titles of the Middle Kingdom*, 3 vols, New York, 1985.

6. R. Hall, *Egyptian textiles*, Aylesbury, 1986, p. 19.

7. Hall, *op. cit.*, p. 18.

8. A.P. Thomas, *Gurob: a New Kingdom town*, Warminster, 1981.

9. Hall, *op. cit.*, p. 16.

10. *P. Lansing*, 8, 4–7; R. Caminos, *Late Egyptian Miscellanies*, London, 1954, 106,15–107,2.

11. L. Manniche, *Sexual life in ancient Egypt*, London, 1987, pp. 106–15.

12. A. Erman, *Life in ancient Egypt*, New York, 1971, p. 295.

13. A.M. Blackman, 'Priest, priesthood (Egyptian)': *Encyclopaedia of religion and ethics*, ed. J. Hastings, Edinburgh, 1908–26, p. 298.

14. N. de Garis Davies & A.H. Gardiner, *The tomb of Amenemhet*, London, 1914, p. 95.

15. B. Watterson, *The gods of ancient Egypt*, London, 1984, pp. 80, 90, 123.

16. K. Sethe, *Urkunden des ägyptischen Altertums*, Leipzig, 1903.

17. H. Hickmann, 'Du battement des mains aux planchettes entrechoquées': *BIÉ*, 37, 1956, pp. 67–122.

18. Lesko, *op. cit.*, p. 20.

19. M. Galvin, 'The hereditary status of the titles of the cult of Hathor': *JEA*, 70, 1984, pp. 42–9.

20. M. Galvin, *The priestesses of Hathor in the Old Kingdom and the First Intermediate Period*, Ann Arbor, 1981.

21. P.E. Newberry, *Beni Hasan*, London, 1893, i, 14, 43.

22. A. Mariette, *Les mastabas de l'ancien empire*, Paris, 1882–9, p. 183.

23. Sethe, *op. cit.*, i, 24 foll.

24. A.H. Gardiner, *ZÄS*, xlv, 127 note 2.

25. *P. Abbott*, 3,17.

26. For the Westcar Papyrus see M. Lichtheim, *Ancient Egyptian Literature*, vol. I, Berkeley and Los Angeles, 1973, pp. 215–22.

27. *P. Cairo dem.* II 30604. For nursing contracts from the Roman period see M.A. Masciadri and O. Montevecchi, 'Contratti di baliatico e vendite fiduciarie a Tebtynis': *Aegyptus*, 62, 1982, pp. 148–61; J. Herrmann, 'Die Ammenvertrage in den grako-ägyptischen papyri': *ZRG*, 76, 1957, pp. 490–9; K.R. Bradley, 'Sexual regulations in wet-nursing contracts from Roman Egypt': *Klio*, 62, 1980, pp. 321–5.

28. B.G. Trigger, *et al.*, *Ancient Egypt: a social history*, Cambridge, 1983, p. 217.

29. M. Werbrouck, *Les pleureuses dans l'Égypte ancienne*, Brussels, 1938.

30. Spencer, *op. cit.*, p. 52.

31. H. Hickmann, 'La danse aux miroirs': *BIÉ*, 37, 1954–5, pp. 151–90.

32. H. Hickmann, 'Die Altaegyptische Rassel': *ZÄS*, 79(ii), 1954, pp. 116–25.

33. M. Lichtheim, *Ancient Egyptian literature*, vol. I, Berkeley and Los Angeles, 1975, p. 220; and A. Erman, *The ancient Egyptians: a sourcebook of their writings*, New York, 1966, p. 44.

34. H. Hickmann, 'Classement et classification des flutes,

clarinettes et hautbois de l'Égypte ancienne': *Cd'É*, 26, 1951, pp. 17–27.

35.   H. Hickmann, 'Les harpes de l'Égypte pharaonique': *BIÉ*, 35, 1953, pp. 309–78; and M. Duchesne-Guillemin, 'Sur la typologie des harpes égyptiennes': *Cd'É*, XLIV No. 87, Jan. 1969, pp. 60–8.

36.   R.D. Anderson, *Catalogue of Egyptian antiquities in the British Museum, III: Musical instruments*, London, 1976, p. 72.

37.   H. Hickmann, 'Les luths aux frettes du Nouvel Empire': *Ann. Serv.*, 52, 1952, pp. 161–83.

38.   H. Hickmann, 'Le tambourin rectangulaire du Nouvel Empire': *Ann. Serv.*, 51, 1951, pp. 317–33.

Bibliography to Chapter Three

Priesthood and temple life

BLACKMAN, A.M., 'Priest, priesthood (Egyptian)': *Encyclopaedia of religion and ethics*, ed. J. Hastings, 13 vols, Edinburgh, 1908–26, pp. 293–302.

—— 'The sequence of episodes in the Egyptian daily temple liturgy': *Journal of the Manchester Egyptian and Oriental Society*, 8, 1919, pp. 27–53.

EVANS, J.A.S., 'A social and economic history of an Egyptian temple in the Graeco-Roman period': *Yale Classical Studies*, No. 17, New Haven, 1961, pp. 149–283.

FAIRMAN, H.W., 'Worship and festival in an Egyptian temple': *Bulletin of the John Rylands Library*, 37, 1954, pp. 165–203.

SAUNERON, S., *The priests of ancient Egypt*, Evergreen Profile Books, 12, 1960.

Music

ANDERSON, R.D., *Catalogue of Egyptian antiquities in the British Museum, III: Musical instruments*, London, 1976.

FARMER, H.G., 'The music of ancient Egypt': *The New Oxford History of music*, vol. 1, ed. Welles, Oxford, 1957, pp. 255–82.

Dancing

BRUNNER-TRAUT, E., 'Der Tanz im alten Ägypten nach bildlichen und inschriftlichen Zeugnissen': *Aegyptologische Forschungen*, Heft 6, Gluckstadt-Hamburg-New York, 1938.

NORD, D., 'The term ẖnr "harem" or "musical performers": *Studies in honor of Dows Dunham*, Boston, 1981, p. 137 foll.

WILD, H., 'Les danses sacrées de l'Égypte ancienne', *Sources Orientales* VI, Paris, 1963.

Notes to Chapter Four

1. See: E.A. Wallis Budge, *Egyptian magic*, London, 1901; F. Lexa, *La magie dans l'Égypte antique de l'ancien empire jusqu'à l'époque copte*, Paris, 1925; C. Jacq, *Egyptian magic*, Warminster, 1985.

2. Ebers Papyrus, 67, 3 *ff* – see Note 5 to Chapter Five.

3. For love poems, see also M. Lichtheim, *Ancient Egyptian literature*, vol. II, Berkley and Los Angeles, 1976, pp. 182–93.

4. For the story of Ahwere and Neneferkaptah, see Lichtheim, *op. cit.*, vol. III, 1980, pp. 127–8.

5. J. Černy, 'Consanguineous marriages in pharaonic Egypt': *JEA*, 40, 1954, pp. 23–9.

6. Herodotus, *The Histories*, III, 32, Penguin Classics, 1965.

7. P.W. Pestman, *Marriage and matrimonial property in ancient Egypt*, Leiden, 1961, p. 7.

8. From Papyrus Chester Beatty I; see Lichtheim, *op. cit.*, vol. II, p. 183.

9. See Lichtheim, *op. cit.*, vol. I, 1975, p. 69 para. 21.

10. B. Adams, *Fragen Altägyptischer Finanzverwaltung*, Munich, 1956, p. 68.

11. Sophocles, *Tereus*, para. 583.

12. William Congreve, *The Way of the World*, iv,v.

13. Pestman, *op. cit.*, p. 52.

14. *ibid.*, p. 11.

15. *P. Louvre* 7846.

16. *P. Berlin* 13614.

17. Pestman, *op. cit.*, p. 9, n. 5.

18. *ibid.*, p. 9, n. 7.

19. *'ḳ r pr*, 'to enter a house in order to marry': 'Adoption papyrus' line 20 (recto); see A.H. Gardiner, 'A Dynasty XX deed of adoption': *JEA*, 26, 1940, p. 23 foll.

20. H. Thompson, *A family archive from Siut*, Oxford, 1934, p. 78.

21. Pestman, *op. cit.*, pp. 12–13.

22. O. Bodleian 253.

23. Pestman, *op. cit.*, p. 11, n. 1.

24. W.F. Edgerton, *Notes on Egyptian marriage, chiefly in the Ptolemaic period*, Chicago, 1931, p. 6–9.

25. Pestman, *op. cit.*, pp. 30–1.

26. *ibid.*, pp. 26–7.

27. *ibid.*, p. 167 foll.

28. *ibid.*, p. 175.

29. *ibid.*, p. 91 foll. A woman's *nktw n sḥmt* usually consisted of beds, vessels of various kinds, mirrors, ornaments, sometimes a musical instrument, especially a *sistrum* (see page 40), or some copper money, and clothing.

30. *inšn*-cloth: the word is often translated as 'shawl'; it was certainly a piece of material, and seems to have had considerable value; see Pestman, *op. cit.*, pp. 94–5.

31. *P. Hausweg*: transcription in W. Erichsen, *Demotische Lesestücke II*, 1, Leipzig, 1937–40, p. 115 foll.

32. Pestman, *op. cit.*, p. 13 foll. and p. 108 foll.

33. *P. Cairo* 50058, 50059 & 50062: see E.A.E. Jelinková, *Cd'É.*, 28, 1953, p. 228 foll.

34. Pestman, *op. cit.*, p. 144 foll.

35. Diodorus I 27 1: for original text and translation see C.H. Oldfather, *Diodorus of Sicily*, Loeb Classical Library, London, 1968.

36. *P. Chicago* 17481; see Pestman, *op. cit.*, p. 32 foll. & p. 102 foll.

37. Lichtheim, *op. cit.*, II, p. 136.

38. H.J. Wolff, *Written and unwritten marriages in Hellenistic and postclassical Roman law*, Haverford, 1939, pp. 70–1.

39. O. Strassburg 1845.

40. Diodorus I 80 3.
41. Herodotus II 92.
42. *P. Mayer A* 13c ll.6–7.
43. W.K. Simpson, 'Polygamy in Egypt in the Middle Kingdom': *JEA*, 60, 1974, pp. 100–5.
44. T. Eric Peet, *The great tomb-robberies of the Twentieth Egyptian Dynasty*, I Text, London, 1930, pp. 156–7.
45. A.H. Gardiner, 'The stela of Amenemhet': *ZÄS*, 47, 1910, p. 92.
46. A.H. Gardiner & K. Sethe, *Egyptian letters to the dead: Papyrus Leiden 371*, London, 1928, reprinted 1975.
47. Herodotus II 111.
48. Diodorus I 78 3–4.
49. A. Erman, *The ancient Egyptians: a sourcebook of their writings*, New York, 1966, pp. 36–8.
50. Pestman, *op. cit.*, pp. 56, 61, 71, 156.
51. Lichtheim, *op. cit.*, III, p. 177, 23 (6–7).
52. *ibid.* p. 169, 13 (12)
53. Erichsen, *op. cit.*, p. 139 foll.
54. J. Černy, *Late Ramesside letters*, Brussels, 1939, 67, 13–68, 1.
55. O. Bodleian 253.
56. *P. Philadelphia* 14.
57. Pestman, *op. cit.*, p. 125 foll.
58. *P. Libbey*

Bibliography to Chapter Four

ALLAM, S., 'Le mariage dans l'Égypte ancienne': *JEA*, 67, 1981, pp. 116–35.

——, 'Quelques aspects du mariage dans l'Égypte ancienne: *JEA*, 67, 1981, pp. 116–35.

el-AMIR, M., *A family archive from Thebes*, Cairo, 1959, p. 138 foll: Further notes on Egyptian marriage and divorce.

EDGERTON, W.F., *Notes on Egyptian marriage, chiefly in the Ptolemaic period*, Chicago, 1931.

EYRE, C.J., 'Crime and adultery in ancient Egypt': *JEA*, 70, 1984, pp. 92–105.

PESTMAN, P.W., *Marriage and matrimonial property in ancient Egypt: a contribution to establishing the legal position of the woman*, Leiden, 1961.

TANNER, R., 'Untersuchungen zur Ehe- und erbrechtlichen Stellung der Frau in pharaonischen Ägypten': *Klio*, 49, 1967, pp. 5–37.

VATIN, C., *Recherches sur le mariage et la condition de la femme mariée à l'époque hellénistique*, Paris, 1970.

Notes to Chapter Five

1. Papyrus Ebers, Spell No. 250 – see note 5 below.
2. A.H. Gardiner and K. Sethe, *Egyptian letters to the dead, Papyrus Leiden*, London, 1928, reprinted 1975.
3. W.R. Dawson, 'The Egyptian medical papyri': E.A. Underwood, ed., *Science, medicine and history*, London, 1953.
4. F.Ll. Griffith, *Hieratic papyri from Kahun and Gurob*, vol. I: Literary, medical and mathematical papyri from Kahun, London, 1898.
5. W. Wreszinski, *Der papyrus Ebers*, Leipzig, 1913; see also B. Ebbell, *The Ebers Papyrus*; and C. Bryan, *Ancient Egyptian medicine: The Papyrus Ebers*, 1974.
6. J.H. Breasted, *The Edwin Smith surgical papyrus*, Chicago, 1930.
7. E. Iversen, *Papyrus Carlsberg No. VIII*, with some remarks on the Egyptian origin of some popular birth prognoses, Copenhagen, 1939.
8. Griffith, *op. cit.*, Case 8.
9. Homer, *The Odyssey*, Book IV, pp. 219–34: trans. E.V. Rieu, Penguin Classics, 1955, p. 70.
10. F. Filce Leek, 'Dental problems during the Old Kingdom – facts and legends': R. David and E. Tapp, *Evidence embalmed: modern medicine and the mummies of ancient Egypt*, Manchester, 1984, pp. 128–9.
11. Wreszinski, *op. cit.*, Nos 739. 740, 743.
12. *ibid.*, No. 98.
13. *ibid.*, No. 853.

14. Griffith, *op. cit.*, Case 11.

15. *ibid.*, Cases 8 & 9.

16. *ibid.*, Case 12.

17. *ibid.*, Case 17.

18. *ibid.*, Case 4.

19. *ibid.*, Case 2.

20. A.T. Sandison, 'Diseases in ancient Egypt': A.& E. Cockburn, *Mummies, disease and ancient cultures*, Cambridge, 1983, p. 31.

21. Griffith, *op. cit.*, Case 5.

22. *ibid.*, Cases 1, 6, 16.

23. G. Majno, *The healing hand: man and wound in the ancient world*, Cambridge, Mass., 1975, p. 115 foll.

24. Celsus, *De Medicinus*, 3 vols, trans. W.G. Spencer, London, 1935–8, vol. II, 8, 30–1.

25. H.V. Williams, 'Human palaeopathology': *Archives of Pathology*, 7, 1929, p. 839.

26. B.M. Willmott Dobbie, *Mediaeval History*, 26, 1982, pp. 79–90. For nineteenth- and twentieth-century statistics on death from post-partum sepsis see E. Shorter, *A history of women's bodies*, London, 1983, pp. 297–317.

27. Griffith, *op. cit.*, Case 26.

28. *ibid.*, Case 27.

29. Hippocrates: *Aphorism*, see: *The medical works of Hippocrates*, trans. by J. Chadwick and W.N. Mann, Oxford, 1950.

30. Griffith, *op. cit.*, Case 28.

31. *ibid.*, Case 20.

32. *ibid.*, Case 18.

33. J. Baines, *Fecundity figures*, Warminster, 1986.

34. Griffith, *op. cit.*, Cases 29 & 31.

35. F. Paullini, *Nue-vermehrte Heilsame Dreckapotheka*, 1697, p. 248.

36. Griffith, *op. cit.*, Cases 21–3.

37. W. Spiegelberg, *Aegyptologisches Randglossar zum Alten Testament*, Strassburg, 1904, p. 19 foll.

38. K. Sethe, *Die altägyptischen Pyramidentexte*, Leipzig, 1908, Para. 1180: determinative of *msḫnt* depicts chair.

39. W.S. Blackman, *The fellahin of Upper Egypt*, London, 1927, p. 63.

40. M. Lichtheim, *Ancient Egyptian literature*, vol. 1, Berkeley and Los Angeles, 1975, pp. 220–1.
41. Wreszinski, *op. cit.*, 97, 13.
42. *ibid.*, 93,17 & 94,9.
43. *ibid.*, 93,3.
44. R.O. Faulkner, *Book of the Dead*, London, 1985, p. 45.
45. W.M.F. Petrie, *Journals*: Entry for April 1889. Kept at University College London.
46. Lichtheim, *op. cit.*, p. 221.

Bibliography to Chapter Five

BROTHWELL, D. and SANDISON, A.T., eds, *Diseases in antiquity*, Springfield, Illinois, 1967.

BUDGE, E., *Herb, doctors and physicians in the ancient world*, London, 1978.

COCKBURN, A.& E., eds, *Mummies, disease and ancient cultures*, Cambridge, 1983.

COLE, D., 'Obstetrics for women in ancient Egypt': *Discussions in Egyptology*, 5, 1986, pp. 27–33.

DAWSON, W., 'Early ideas concerning contraception': *Medical help on birth control*, London, 1928, pp. 189–200.

GHALIOUNGUI, P., *Magic and medical science in ancient Egypt*, London, 1963.

——, *The house of life, per ankh: magic and medical science in ancient Egypt*, Amsterdam, 1973.

——, *The physicians of pharaonic Egypt*, Cairo, 1983.

GRAPOW, H., *Grundriss der Medizin der alten Ägypter*, Berlin, 1954.

HIMES, N.E., *Medical history of contraception*, Baltimore, 1936.

JACKSON, R., *Doctors and diseases in the Roman Empire*, London, 1988.

LECA, A.P., *La médicine Égyptienne aux temps des pharaons*, 1983.

MANNICHE, L., *An ancient Egyptian herbal*, London, 1989.

PINCH, G., 'Childbirth and female figurines at Deir el-Medina and el-Amarna': *Orientalia*, 52, 1983, ,pp. 405–14.

STEVENS, J.M., 'Gynaecology from ancient Egypt': *Medical Journal of Australia*, 2, 1975, pp. 949–52.

Notes to Chapter Six

1. E.J. Baumgartel, *Predynastic Egypt, CAH* I, IX(a), 1965, p. 9.
2. *ibid.*
3. Herodotus, *The Histories*, II, 80.
4. R. Hall, *Egyptian textiles*, Aylesbury, 1986, p. 10.
5. For a description of linen-making see: T.G.H. James,
   An introduction to ancient Egypt, London, 1979, pp. 235–6.
6. E. Riefstahl, *Patterned textiles in pharaonic Egypt*, Brooklyn,
   1944.
7. R.M. Hall, Two linen dresses from the Fifth Dynasty site of
   Deshasheh now in the Petrie Museum of Egyptian Archae-
   ology, University College London: *JEA*, 67, 1981,
   pp. 168–71; R.M. Hall and L. Pedrini, A pleated linen dress
   from a Sixth Dynasty tomb at Gebelein now in the Museo
   Egizio, Turin: *JEA*, 70, 1984, pp. 136–9.
8. W.M.F. Petrie, *Tarkhan II*, London, 1914.
9. J.H. Breasted, Jr, *Egyptian servant statues*, Washington, 1948.
10. R. Hall, *Egyptian textiles*, Aylesbury, 1986, p. 55.
11. Riefstahl, *op. cit.*, pp. 11–15.
12. Hall, *op. cit.*, p. 55.
13. J. Stevens Cox, The construction of an ancient Egyptian wig
    (*c*. 1400 BC) in the British Museum: *JEA*, 63, 1977,
    pp. 67–70.
14. C.A.R. Andrews, *Catalogue of Egyptian antiquities in the British
    Museum, VI, Jewellery: From the earliest times to the Seventeenth
    Dynasty*, London, 1981.
15. C. Aldred, *Jewels of the pharaohs*, London, 1971, p. 35.
16. W. Wreszinski, *Der papyrus Ebers*, Leipzig, 1913, Spell Nos
    65, 8, 16, 19; 66, 1.
17. *op. cit.* 66, 9, 15, 20, 21.
18. *op. cit.* 67, 3 ff.
19. *op. cit.* 47, 19.
20. *op. cit.* 66, 9, 20, 15, 21.
21. *op. cit.* 65, 8, 16; 66, 1.
22. B. Adams, *Egyptian mummies*, Aylesbury, 1984, pp. 35–6.
23. H.E. Winlock, *Excavations at Deir el Bahri*, New York, 1942.

Bibliography to Chapter Six

ADAMS, B., *Predynastic Egypt*, Aylesbury, 1988.

ALDRED, C., *Jewels of the pharaohs*, London, 1971.

ANDREWS, C., *Ancient Egyptian jewellery*, London, 1991.

BAUMGARTEL, E., *The cultures of predynastic Egypt*, Oxford, vol. I, 1955; vol. II, 1960.

HOFFMAN, M.A., *Egypt before the pharaohs*, London, 1984.

LILYQUIST, C., *Ancient Egyptian mirrors from the earliest times through the Middle Kingdom*, Münchner Ägyptologische Studien, Heft 27, 1979.

RIEFSTAHL, E., *Toilet articles from ancient Egypt*, from the Charles Edwin Wilbour Memorial Collection and the Collection of the New York Historical Society in the Brooklyn Museum, Brooklyn, 1943.

STAELIN, E., *Untersuchungen zur ägyptischen Tracht im Alten Reich*, Berlin, 1966.

VILIMKOVA, M., *Egyptian jewellery*, London, 1969.

WILKINSON, A., *Ancient Egyptian jewellery*, London, 1971.

Notes to Chapter Seven

1. M. Lichtheim, *Ancient Egyptian literature*, vol. II, Berkeley, 1976, p. 141.

2. W.S. Blackman, *The fellahin of Upper Egypt*, London, 1927, p. 45.

3. S.B. Pomeroy, *Goddesses, whores, wives and slaves: Women in classical antiquity*, New York, 1975. For examples of infant exposure see pp. 36, 40, 46, 69–70, 127, 140, 164, 228.
   ——, 'Infanticide in hellenistic Greece': *Images of women in antiquity*, ed. A. Cameron & A. Kuhrt, London, 1983, pp. 207–22.

4. Posidippus, Hermaphroditus, frag. 11.

5. *P. Oxyrhynchus* 744.

6. Theban Tomb No. 69.

7. Theban Tomb No. 34.

8. B.M. Bryan, 'Evidence of female literacy from Theban tombs of the New Kingdom', *Bes*, 6, 1984, pp. 17–32.

9. *P. Anastasi*, iii: see A. Erman, *The ancient Egyptians*, New York, 1966, p. 189.

10. A.R. David, 'Toys and games': *The pyramid builders of ancient Egypt*, London, 1986, pp. 162–4.

11. Herodotus, *The Histories*, II, 96, Harmondsworth, 1965.

12. Herodotus, *op. cit.*, 35.

13. R. Hall, *Egyptian textiles*, Aylesbury, 1986, p. 48.

14. Herodotus, *op. cit.*, 93.

Bibliography to Chapter Seven

ALLAM, S., *Some pages from everyday life in ancient Egypt*, Cairo, 1986.

BIERBRIER, M.L., *The tomb-builders of the pharaohs*, London, 1982.

BOSTON MUSEUM OF FINE ARTS, *Egypt's golden age: The art of living in the New Kingdom 1558–1085 BC*, Boston, 1981.

ČERNY, J., *A community of workmen at Thebes in the Ramesside period*, Cairo, 1973.

ERMAN, A., *Life in ancient Egypt*, New York, 1971.

JANSSEN, R. & J., *Egyptian household animals*, Aylesbury, 1989.

——, *Growing up in ancient Egypt*, London, 1990.

MONTET, P., *Everyday life in ancient Egypt in the days of Ramesses the Great*, London, 1958.

ROMER, J., *Ancient lives*, London, 1984.

STEAD, M., *Egyptian life*, London, 1986.

UPHILL, E.P., *Egyptian towns and cities*, Aylesbury, 1988.

WENIG, S., *La femme dans l'ancienne Égypte*, Leipzig, 1967.

WHALE, S., *The family in the Eighteenth Dynasty of Egypt*, Sydney, 1989.

WILSON, H., *Egyptian food and drink*, Aylesbury, 1988.

Notes to Chapter Eight

1. Herodotus, *The Histories*, II, pp. 100–1.

2. A. Gardiner, *Egypt of the Pharaohs*, Oxford, 1961, p. 141.

3. P.G. Elgood, *The Ptolemies of Egypt*, Bristol, 1938, p. vii.

4. William Shakespeare, *Antony and Cleopatra*, Act II, Scene 2.

5. W.L. Rodgers, *Greek and Roman naval warfare*, Annapolis, 1937, p. 535.

6. P.W. Sergeant, 1909.

7. H. Volkmann, 1958.

8. O. von Wertheimer, 1931.

9. One head is in the Cherchell Museum, the other in Antikensammlung, Berlin.

10. Plutarch, *Lives of the Noble Romans*.

11. Breasted, *ARE*, ii, pp. 33–7, Chicago, 1906.

12. *ARE*, ii, pp. 29–32.

13. J.A. Knudtzen, *Die El-Amarna-Tafeln*, 2 vols, Leipzig, 1908–15, Letter 26. See also S. Mercer, *The Tell el Amarna Tablets*, 2 vols, Toronto, 1939.

14. J. Gohary, 'Nefertiti at Karnak': J. Ruffle *et al.*, ed., *Glimpses of ancient Egypt*, Warminster, 1979, pp. 30–1. See also J. Samson, *Amarna, city of Akhenaten: Nefertiti as pharaoh*, London, 1978; and N. Reeves, *The complete Tutankhamun*, London, 1990, pp. 22–3, for an outline of the theory that Nefertiti is to be identified with Smenkare.

15. *JEA*, xli, p. 83 foll.

16. G. Robins, in A. Cameron and A. Kuhrt, ed., *Images of Women in antiquity*, London, 1983.

17. C.E. Sander-Hansen, *Das Gottesweib des Amun*, Copenhagen, 1940.

18. B.M. No. 46699.

19. W. Murnane, *United with eternity*, Chicago, 1980, p. 82.

20. Nahum 3: 8–10.

21. *ARE*, iv, pp. 901–16.

22. Theban Tomb No. 34.

23. H. Legrain, *Ann. Serv.*, vii, 1906, pp. 226–7.

24. R. Caminos, 'The Adoption Stele of Nitocris': *JEA*, 50, 1964.

25. J. Leclant, *Journal of Near Eastern Studies*, xiii, 1954, p. 169.

26. *ARE*, iv, pp. 935–58.

27. Theban Tomb No. 279.

28. L.A. Christophe, 'Les trois derniers grands majordomes de

la XXVIe Dynastie': *Ann. Serv.*, LIV, 1956, pp. 83–100.

29. *ARE*, 958 F,G.
30. *ARE*, iv, 988 D.
31. G. Maspero, 'Deux monuments de la princesse Ankhnasnifiribri': *Ann. Serv.*, V, 1904, p. 84 foll.
32. B.M. No. 32.
33. C.E. Sander-Hansen, *Die religiosen Texte auf den Sarg der Anchnesneferibre neu*, Copenhagen, 1957.

Bibliography to Chapter Eight

ALDRED, C., *Akhenaten and Nefertiti*, Brooklyn, 1973.

——, *Akhenaten, King of Egypt*, London, 1986.

——, *Akhenaten, Pharaoh of Egypt*, London, 1968.

BRADFORD, E, *Cleopatra*, London, 1971.

ELGOOD, P.G., *The Ptolemies of Egypt*, Bristol, 1938.

GARDINER, A.H, *Egypt of the pharaohs*, Oxford, 1961.

GITTON, M., *Les Divines Épouses de la 18e*, Paris, 1984.

GOHARY, J., *Akhenaten's Sed-festival at Karnak*, London, 1991.

GRAEFE., *Untersuchungen zur Verwaltung und Geschichte der Institution der Gottesgemahlin des Amun vom Beginnn des Neuen Reiches bis zur Spatzeit*, Wiesbaden, 1981.

GYLES, M.F., *Pharaonic policies and administration, 663 to 323 BC*, Univ. N. Carolina Press, 1959.

HALLETT, L.H-., *Cleopatra: Histories, dreams and distortions*, London, 1990.

KITCHEN, K.A., *Pharaoh triumphant*, Warminster, 1983.

——, *The Third Intermediate Period in Egypt (1100–650 BC)*, 2nd ed. rev., Warminster, 1986.

MARTIN, G.T., *The royal tomb at El-'Amarna II*, London, 1989.

REDFORD, B., *Akhenaten: The heretic king*, Princeton, 1984.

SAMSON, J., *Nefertiti and Cleopatra*, London, 1985.

WEIGALL, A., *The life and times of Cleopatra, Queen of Egypt*, London, 1923.

INDEX OF ANCIENT EGYPTIAN WORDS AND PHRASES

3šr, 133

ìì, 117
ìw.s m ḥmt n, 62
ìw.s m-dì, 62
ìpt, 25, 127
ìnšn, 64
ìrì n ḥmt, 60
ìt, 87

'n ḥmt, 62
'k r pr, 60

w'bw, 39
'bw Shmt, 74
w'bt Ḥwt-ḥr, 42

bdt, 87

pr nṯr, 39
psì, 133

fsì, 133

m33t Ḥr Sth, 148
m33tt, 89
mìmì, 89
mwt msw nìswt, 148

mwt nṯr, 148
mb', 91
mnì, 60, 61
mrt, 42
mrt.f, 62
mshnt, 90
msdmt, 116
mdw n '3w, 121

ny, 91
nbt ḥwt, 62
nrw phwt, 74
nkwt n shmt, 64, 71

rht-nsw, 42
rdì n A B m ḥmt, 59, 60

h3y, 62
hy, 62
hk3t, 131

ḥwt nṯr, 39
ḥbsyt, 62
ḥm nṯr, 39, 40
ḥm-k3, 40
ḥmsì r-', 60
ḥmt, 62
ḥmt.f ḥr-h3t, 67

ḥmt nsw wrt, 148
ḥmt nṯr, 42, 148
ḥnwt, 40
ḥnyt, 40
ḥd, 107

hnmwt, 38
hkrt-nsw-w'tt, 42

s3, 43
sìnw, 74
sìnw ìbḥ, 74, 78
sìnw ìrt, 74
sìnw ḥt, 74
sm3wt nbwy, 148
sh n ḥmt, 62, 63
sh n s'nḥ, 65
sdm, 115

šp n shmt, 64, 65, 71
šm'wt, 40
šm'wt n 'Imn, 43

kfn, 133

grg pr, 60

dm' n ḥmt, 62

GENERAL INDEX

Abu Simbel, 156
Abydos, Tetisheri monuments, 149
Actium, Battle of, 144, 145
adoption, 32
Adorer of the God (title), 43
adultery, 69, 70
Aegyptiaca, 137
Afterlife, 2
Ahhotep, 106, 149, 150
Ahmose, king, 149
Ahmose, queen, 140; valour of, 149
Ahmose, vizier, 139
Ahmose-Nefertiry, 115, 149, 150
— patron of tomb-workers, 150
Ahwere, 56, 60
Akhemenron, 168
Akhenaten, 153
Akhetaten, 153
Alexander Helios, 143
Alexander the Great, xi, 141
alopecia, 77, 111
Amarna Period, 104, 110, 152, 159
Amasis, 170
Amenhotep I, 150
Amenhotep III, 151
Amenhotep IV, 151, 152, 153
Amenirdis I, 162, 163, 164
— adoption by Divine Wife of Amun, 162
— mortuary chapel, Medinet Habu, 163, 164, 171
Amenirdis II, 163, 167, 168
— adoption by Divine Wife of Amun, 163, 167
— return to Kush, 168
amulets, 93, 104, 105, 106, 108
Amun, 17, 139, 140
— cult of, 153
Amun, Divine Wife of, *see under* Divine Wife of Amun
Amun, High Priest of, 157, 158

Amun, High Priestess of, 43
Amun, Oracle of, 157, 161
Anastasi Papyrus, 79
anaesthesia, 83
Anat, 17
Ani, 12, 66, 120, 121
ankh-sign, 104
Ankhesenamun, 154
Ankhesenpaaten, 154
Ankhnesmeryre, 5
Ankhnesneferibre, 161, 170; First Prophet of Amun, 170
— adoption by Divine Wife of Amun, 169, 171
— mortuary chapel, Medinet Habu, 170
— sarcophagus, 170, 171
Ankhsheshonq, 12, 58, 70
anklets, 105, 108
antibiotics, 83
antisepsis, 91
Antony, Mark, 141, 142
aphrodisiacs, 76, 78, 86
Apollonia, 28, 29, 30
Apries, 169
Apuleius, 21
armlets, 108, 109
aroura (Greek) – 0.68 acres
Arsinoe, sister of Cleopatra VII, 142
art, conventions of, 4; purposes of, 3
artaba (Greek) – 30 kilos
Assurbanipal of Assyria, 165
Astarte, 21
Aten, 152, 153, 154
Atum, 17
Ay, 154

Badarians, 94
bad breath, 79
baking *see under* domestic activities
baldness, 111

balls, used in dancing, 47
bangles, 105, 108
banquets, 135
Bastet, 17, 21
Bay, chancellor, 140
beads, 105, 106
beauty, ideals of, 9, 102
beauty treatment, 78, 111
beer, 130, 131
belts, 105, 109
Berenike, sister of Cleopatra VII, 141
Berlin Papyrus, 76, 85, 86, 87, 89
Bes, 93, 116
Binothris, 138
birth stool, 44, 90
Blackman, Winifred S., xiii, xiv, 121
bracelets, 105, 106, 107, 108
bread, 78, 129, 130
Breasted, J.H., 76
breast-feeding, 88, 91, 123
brewing *see under* domestic activities
broad-collars *see* collars
burial, 24
byssus, 96

Caesarion, 141
Cambyses, 57, 170
cancer, 76, 81
Canopic jars, 18
Carlsberg VIII Papyrus, 76, 86, 87, 88
castanets, 47, 49
cats, 135
Celsus, 84
characteristics, female, 2
Chester Beatty Papyrus, 76
childbirth, 26, 44, 76, 80, 84, 90
children, 120, 121, 122
chokers, 108
Cicero, 46
civil status of women, 37
cleanliness, personal, 117
Clement of Alexandria, 75
Cleopatra VII, 141 foll.
— in drama, 143, 145
— personal attributes, 145 foll.
Cleopatra Selene, 143
climate, 94
cloaks, 99
clothing, 94, 95
collars, 106, 108

combs, 113
concubinage, 68
concubines, royal, 148
contraception, 75, 76, 88, 89
cooking *see under* domestic activities
corsetry, 102
cosmetic jars, 116, 119
cosmetics, 115
cotton, 95
creator gods, 17
crowns, 110

Dahshur jewellery, 106, 109, 110
dancing, 38, 46, 47, 49, 53
deben – 91 grammes
Deir el-Bahri, 140
demotic, x, 13
dentistry, 78, 79
dentists, 78
deodorants, 117
depilation, 117
depression, 80
Destruction of Mankind, 18
diadems, 110
diet, 129 foll.
Diodorus Siculus, xi, xii, 65, 67, 69, 131
Dion Cassius, 144
disinheritance, 33
Divine Votaress, 158, 160
Divine Wife of Amun, 43, 158, 159 foll.
— adoption, 160, 162, 163, 167, 169, 171
— mortuary chapels, Medinet Habu, 160, 162, 163, 164, 170, 171
— officials of, 168
— power of, 171
— wealth of, 160, 161, 168
divorce, 67, 70, 71, 72
djed-column, 104
DNA, x
doctors, 73, 74
dogs, 135
domestic activities, 35, 133
Doomed Prince, The, 16
dowries, 64, 71, 122
dresses, 97, 99
drugs, medicinal, 82, 83
drums, 49
Dryton, 29, 30, 31
dyeing, 96
dynasties, 137

ear-plugs, 110
earrings, 108, 109
ear-studs, 110
Earth god, 17
Ebers Papyrus, 75, 79, 80, 81, 88, 89, 90, 91,
    111, 112, 127
Edjo, 17, 145
education, 124
electrum, 107
embroidery, 97
erotica, 8, 38
Esarhaddon, 165, 166
Esemkhebe, 158
exposure of infants, 122
eye make-up, 115, 116
Eye of Horus amulet, 104

false teeth, 78, 79
families, 120
family planning, 88
famine, 129
fashion, 98
feminine ailments, 80
fertility, 85, 86
fertility deities, 17
fertility figures, 86
fertility tests, 76, 85
fiscus-dues, 30
flax, 95
flutes, 49, 50, 52
Fly, Order of the Golden, 149
food, preparation of, 35, 126, 128, 129
fuel, 133
— collection of, 36
Fulvia, 143
funerary deities, 17

games, 125, 134
Geb, 17
Gilukhepa, 151
girdles, 105, 109
gleaning, 27
goddesses, 17
gold, 107
Golden Ass, The, 21
gonorrhea, 75, 80
Great Royal Wife, 148, 149, 151, 156
guardians, 25, 26, 30
gynaeceum, 25
gynaecology, 75, 76

hair, 111, 112, 113, 115
haircolour, 113
hairdressing, 113
hairpieces, 102
halitosis, 80
Hand of the God (title), 43, 160
Hapusoneb, 139
harem, 127
Harem Conspiracy, 157
harlots, 13
harpers, blind, 52
harps, 49, 50, 52
harvesting, 27, 36
Hathor, 17, 18, 19, 39, 40, 86, 92, 119
— coiffure, 102
— cult of, 42, 43
Hatshepsut, 138 foll., 156, 159
— divine birth, 140
— mortuary temple, Deir el-Bahri, 140
— obelisks, 139
— statues of, 140
— tomb, 140
health problems, 73, 77
heiress, royal *see under* royal heiress
Hekat, 44, 90
henna, 113
hens, 132
Henttowy, 158
Herakleopolis, 165, 167
herbs, 132, 133
Herihor, 157
Herodotus, xi, 25, 67, 68, 127, 128, 129, 138
Hetepheres, 106, 107, 119
Hippocrates, 85
Hittites, 152
honey, 132
Horemheb, 154
Horus, 17, 19, 138
house cleaning, 127
household remedies, 78
houses, 125, 126
Hyksos, 149

ibe, 168, 169
illiteracy, 35
Infant Jesus, iconography of, 31
infant mortality, 84
infidelity, 68
inheritance, 32
Insinger Papyrus, 13
Intermediate Periods, 137: 1st, *c.* 2181–2134 BC;

2nd, 1786–1551 BC; 3rd, 1085–715 BC
Isis, 17, 18, 19, 20, 21, 40, 44, 90
— popularity of, 21
— temple of, 20

jewellery, 104 foll.
Julius Africanus, 137, 138
Julius Caesar, 141, 142

Kadashman-Enlil of Babylon, 151
Kahun Papyrus, 75, 76, 80, 81, 82, 85, 86, 87, 88
Kahun (site), 92
— jewellery, 106, 109, 110
Kamose, 149
Kawit, 113
Kemuny, 119
Khamwese and Tabubu, 15
Khentkawes, 148
kingship, 138
kite – 10 grammes approx.
kohl, 116
kyphi, 118
kyrios (Greek), *see under* guardians

labour (in childbirth), 90
Lahun *see under* Kahun
land tenure, 24
Late Period (715–343 BC), 157
laundry, 27, 128
laundry lists, 99
lavatory-stool, Amarna, 126
law, women's rights under, 27
legal rights of women, 1, 27
legal status of women, 24
leisure, 134
life expectancy, 58, 84
linen, 95, 96, 99, 128
linen, royal (*byssus*), 96
lip-salve, 116
lipstick, 116
loans, 31
loincloths, 101, 128
love, 17, 54
love poetry, 8, 10, 11, 54, foll.
lutes, 50, 51, 52, 53
Luxor temple, statue groups, 6
lyres, 50

Maat, 18
magic, 54, 73, 74; sympathetic magic, 74, 90

magicians, 73, 74
maintenance document, 65
Makare, 158, 159
malachite, 115
Manetho, 137, 138, 140
market, going to, 27, 35
marriage, 57 foll.
— age at, 58
— attitude towards, 59
— between brother and sister, 57
— between father and daughter, 151, 154, 155
— customs, 59
— Muslim, 61
— trial, 66
— types of, 62
marriages, arranged, 57
marriage contract *see* marriage settlement
marriage settlement, 61, 63, 64, 65
Married Women's Property Act, 31
Mary *see under* Virgin Mary
matrilineal descent, 23
medical complaints, 73, 77
medical papyri, 75; *see also under*: Anastasi; Berlin; Carlsberg VIII; Chester Beatty; Ebers; Kahun; Ramesseum; Smith, Edwin
medical service, 74
medicine, 44, 73
medimnus, 26
Medinet Habu, 6, 160, 162, 163, 164, 170, 171
Mehytenweskhet, 170
Menander, 25
menit-necklace, 40, 49
menstruation, 80, 81, 84
Mereruka and wife, 53
Meresankh, 43
Meritaten, 154
Meskhenet, 44
mice as medicine, 91
Middle Kingdom (*c.* 2134–1633 BC), 137
midwifery, 38, 43
— school of, 43
midwives, 43, 44, 84, 89
Min, 17
mirror-cases, 119
mirrors, 118, 119
— in dancing, 47
miscarriage, 80
Mitanni, 151
Mithras, 21

molecular cloning, x
monkeys, 135
Montu, 17
Montuemhet, 123, 166, 167
— tomb of, 166
morning after pill, 89
mortality rates, 44, 84
mortuary offerings, 37
mortuary priests, 37
mortuary temple of Hatshepsut, 140
Mose, 33, 34
mothers, 13, 120, 121
mourners, professional, 45
mourning, 38, 45
mummification, x
music, 38, 49
musicians, 40, 49, 51, 53
Mutemhab, 67
Mutnodjmet, 154

names, personal, 92
Naqada I, 105
Naqada II, 105
Naunakhte, 33
Nebnofret, 34
Necho II, 169
Necho of Sais, 165
necklaces, 105, 106, 108
Nefertiri,
— mortuary temple, 155
— tomb, 155
Nefertiti, 135, 151, 152, 159; and the Aten,
    154
Neferu, 113
Neferure, 139, 156, 159
Neith, 17, 39
— cult of, 43
— school of midwifery, 43
Nekhbet, 17
Nenefer, adoption of, 32
Nephthys, 40, 44, 90
Neskhons, 158
New Kingdom (1551–1085 BC), 137
Nitocris, 138, 161, 166, 167, 169
— adoption by Divine Wife, 167
— death of, 170
— mortuary chapel, Medinet Habu, 170
— officials of, 168, 169
— sarcophagus of, 170
— wealth of, 168
Nut, 17, 21

obelisks of Hatshepsut, 139
obscenity, 7
Octavia, 143
Octavianus, 142, 144
Old Kingdom (c. 2686–2181 BC), 137
Opening of the Mouth Ceremony, 2
Oracle of Amun *see under* Amun
Order of the Golden Fly, 149
Osiris, 17, 18, 40
Osiris, Ruler of Eternity, temple of, 162
Osorkon III, 159, 162
ostraca, x

Pabasa, 168
paddle dolls, 100
Padihorresnet, 169
Padineith, 170
Pakhet, cult of, 43
palettes, 115
papyri, x
papyrus, medical, *see under* medical papyri
papyrus, obscene, 7
Paullini, 88
pendants, 105, 106, 108
Pepi II, 138
perfumes, 117
Persian rule in Egypt, xi, 140
pests, 127, 128
Petrie, W.M.F., xi, 92, 97
pets, 135
Philae, temple of Isis, 20
Philippi, Battle of, 142, 143
Piankh, 158
Piankhi, 162
Pinudjem I, 158
Pinudjem II, 158
pipes, 50, 53
placenta, 91
pleating, 99, 100
Pliny, 118
Plutarch, 146, 147
poetry *see under* love poetry
polyandry, 67
polygamy, 62, 67
Posidippus, 122
Potiphar's wife, 15
pregnancy, 75
pregnancy tests, 86
priestesses, 39, 40
— status of, 41
priesthood, 38

priests, 39
princesses, foreign, 151
professions, female, 38
prolapse, uterine, 81
property, acquisition of, 31; administration of, 24; inheritance of, 23; rights to, 24
prostitution, 38
Psammetichus I, xi, 165, 166, 167, 169
Psammetichus II, 169
Psammetichus III, 162
Ptah, 17
Ptahhotep, 12, 58, 65
Ptolemaic Dynasty (304–30 BC), xi, 25, 28, 141
Ptolemy I (Lagides), 141
Ptolemy II Philadelphus, 143
Ptolemy XII Auletes, 141
Ptolemy XIII, 141
public office, 37
Punt expedition, 139
purification after childbirth, 92

queens *see under* wives, royal
queens regnant, 138 foll.

Ramesses II, 155
— daughters of, 6
Ramesses III, conspiracy against, 157; queens of, 6
Ramesses XI, 157
Ramesseum Papyri, 76, 88, 89
Ramose, tomb robber, 67
rattles, 49
Re, 17, 44
Reddjedet, 44, 53, 90, 92
religion, Egyptian, 17
Renenutet, 17, 21
respect towards wives, 62
rings, 105, 108
royal heiress, 23, 148, 156
royal wives *see under* wives, royal

s3-sign, 104
sandals, 102
Sebtitis, 28
Sekhmet, 17, 18, 74
self-enslavement, 33
Semtutefnakhte, 167
Senebtisi, jewellery, 110
Senenmut, 139, 140
senet (game), 134

Senmen, 139
Senmonthis *see* Apollonia
Sennuwy, Lady, 4
Seqenenre Tao I, 149
Seqenenre Tao II, 149
Serket, 17, 18
servants, 125
Seshat, 18
Seth, 19
Seti II, 140
'sewerage pharmacology', 83, 111
sewing, 98
sex, ascertaining before birth, 75, 87, 88
sexuality, 86
Shepenwepet I, 162
— mortuary chapel, Medinet Habu, 162
Shepenwepet II, 163, 165, 167, 170
— adoption by Divine Wife, 163
— mortuary chapel, Medinet Habu, 170
Sheshonq, son of Harsiese, 169, 170
Sheshonq, son of Padineith, 170
Shuttarna of Mitanni, 151
silk, 95
silver, 107
singing, 49
Siptah, 140
sistrum, 8, 40, 49
Sitamun, 151
Sit-Hathor-Iunet, jewellery, 109, 110
skin blemishes, 117
skirts, 101
slavery, 32
sleepers (for ears), 110
sleeves, 99
Smenkare, 154
Smith, Edwin, Papyrus, 76, 78, 81, 91
Sobek, 17
Sobekneferu, 138
social position of women, 27
Solon, 24
Sothis, 21
Sponnesis, 44
spoons, cosmetic, 118
status, civil, 37
sterility, 75
Strabo, xi, xii, 122
Suppiluliumash, 154
surgery, 76
surgical treatment, 77
sympathetic magic, 74, 90
syphilis, 80

Tadukhepa, 151
Taharqa, 163, 165, 166
Takeloth III, 162
tambourines, 47, 49, 53
Tanis, 157
Tantamani, 165, 167
Tarkhan, 97, 99
Tarkhundaradu of Arzawa, 151
Tarsus, 143
tattooing, 116
Tausert, 159
Taweret, 92
teeth, 78; cleaning of, 79
temples, cult, 5; mortuary, 5; reliefs, 5; *see also under* Abu Simbel, Abydos, Deir el-Bahri, Medinet Habu
Tetisheri, 115, 149, 150; honours bestowed upon, 149
Theban necropolis, 157
Thebes, sack of, 165
Thoth, 135
— cult of, 43
Tiy, 151, 154, 159
toys, 125
training, dancers, 47; medical, 43, 44, 74
trial marriage, 66
Tushratta of Mitanni, 151
Tutankhamun, 154; jewellery, 106, 107
Tuthmosis I, 140
Tuthmosis III, 99, 139, 140, 153
— queens' jewellery, 109, 110
Tuyu, 151
Two Brothers, Story of the, 15, 69
Twosret, 140; tomb of, 140
tyt-sign, 104

umbilical cord, 91
underwear, 101, 128

unguents, 117, 118
urine tests, 88
uterus, prolapse of, 75

venereal disease, 75, 80, 82
verdict (in medical papyri), 82
Virgin Mary, iconography of, 21
Votaress see Divine Votaress

el-walad et-tani (Arabic), 91
water carrying, 36
weaving, 27, 38, 96
Werirenptah, 51
Wernero, 33
Westcar Papyrus, 14, 44, 49, 69, 90, 91, 92
wet-nurses, 44, 45, 91
wigs, 102, 103, 104, 113; ornaments for, 108, 110
Wilbour Papyrus, 24
wine, 131
winnowing, 27
Wisdom Instructions, 12, 13
Wisdom Texts see Wisdom Instructions
wives, 13; respect for, 62
wives, royal, 148 foll.; Great Royal Wives, 148, 149, 151, 156
women, characteristics of, 2, 13; ideals of beauty, 9; legal status, 24; sexual objects, 7
wool, 95
wrinkles, cure for, 78, 117
writing, goddess of, 18

'year of eating', 66
Yuya, 151

Zananzash, 154

20 ROJ½